James Cawthorn, George Austen and The Curious Case of the Schoolboy Who was Killed

James Cawthorn, George Austen and
The Curious Case of the Schoolboy Who was Killed

James Cawthorn,
George Austen
and

The Curious Case of the Schoolboy Who was Killed

The story behind the first library
built at Tonbridge School

MARTIN J CAWTHORNE

Copyright © 2017 Martin J Cawthorne

The moral right of the author has been asserted.

Apart from any fair dealing for the purposes of research or private study, or criticism or review, as permitted under the Copyright, Designs and Patents Act 1988, this publication may only be reproduced, stored or transmitted, in any form or by any means, with the prior permission in writing of the publishers, or in the case of reprographic reproduction in accordance with the terms of licences issued by the Copyright Licensing Agency. Enquiries concerning reproduction outside those terms should be sent to the publishers.

Matador
9 Priory Business Park,
Wistow Road, Kibworth Beauchamp,
Leicestershire. LE8 0RX
Tel: 0116 279 2299
Email: books@troubador.co.uk
Web: www.troubador.co.uk/matador
Twitter: @matadorbooks

ISBN PB: 978 1785898 600
HB: 978 1785899 164

British Library Cataloguing in Publication Data.
A catalogue record for this book is available from the British Library.

Printed and bound by CPI Group (UK) Ltd, Croydon, CR0 4YY
Typeset in 11pt Minion Pro by Troubador Publishing Ltd, Leicester, UK

Matador is an imprint of Troubador Publishing Ltd

MIX
Paper from responsible sources
FSC® C013604

ACKNOWLEDGMENTS

I would first like to acknowledge the support of my family in helping me to write this book. My wife for her constant and unfailing patience and encouragement; my daughter for always coming up with a suggestion about how to take my research forward whenever I encountered a blind alley or was unsure about how to proceed; and my two teenage sons for always keeping my feet firmly on the ground through their utter indifference to their father's interest in the past.

Secondly, I would like to thank the scores of archivists, historians and librarians I have had the privilege and pleasure to meet during my research. They are too numerous to mention in person but that does not belittle or lessen my admiration for their professionalism, helpfulness and sheer enthusiasm for their work. They are a remarkable group of people and without them it would be impossible to write a book such as this.

Finally, I would like to thank Tonbridge School for the support and encouragement I have received, particularly from Andrew Mayer amongst the Governors; the Headmaster, Tim Haynes; and the Chairman of the Old Tonbridgians, David Walsh.

All and any errors and omissions in the book are, of course, entirely my own responsibility.

All reasonable efforts have been made to ensure that, where necessary, permisson has been obtained to quote relevant source material and appropriate references have been made. In particular the author wishes to express his thanks and gratitude to the Worshipful Company of Skinners for their permission to use the Company's archives deposited at the London Metropolitian Archives (Guildhall Library).

CONTENTS

Foreword		ix
Preface		xiii
Introduction		xv
Chapter One	– The Death of a Schoolboy	1
Chapter Two	– Reports of another Curious Death	23
Chapter Three	– Building Foundations	29
Chapter Four	– Building the Library	60
Chapter Five	– Developing Literary Connections	84
Chapter Six	– From Rule Books to School Books	106
Chapter Seven	– Cawthorn's Legacy	124
Chapter Eight	– Austen's Legacy	138
Chapter Nine	– Enduring Legacies	162
Chapter Ten	– Making Sense of the Enigma	168
Notes and References		186
Bibliography		212
Index		220

FOREWORD

By Tim Haynes, Headmaster of Tonbridge School

James Cawthorn is an important part of the history of Tonbridge School, which was founded in 1553 by Sir Andrew Judd. Cawthorn became, in 1743, its fourteenth headmaster and I have the privilege of being the thirty-first. There exists a very strong sense of continuity from Cawthorn's time to ours. The school occupies the same site as on the day of its foundation; the Skinners' Company, an increasingly powerful force in the present for educational advancement, continues to provide the stewardship and governance of the school as it has done since Sir Andrew Judd, in his will, entrusted the school to its care. The Judd Foundation benefits, through bursaries and scholarships, many boys who would not otherwise be able to benefit from a Tonbridge education.

In the published histories of the school, Cawthorn receives a distinctly adverse press as a severe disciplinarian who locked a boy in a cupboard, and then forgot about him, so that the boy starved to death. In David Somervell's History of Tonbridge School the story is dismissed as a myth, but mud sticks. Headmasters can sometimes be misrepresented, so Martin Cawthorne is to be commended on restoring his ancestor's reputation.

The more lasting and important achievement of Cawthorn was the establishment of a magnificent library through which the education of his pupils could be focused. The original books are still lovingly preserved by the school and, when last valued, it was said of them: "The real value of the library is a cumulative and contextual one. The interest and importance of the collection lies in its age and cohesiveness. The library as a whole constitutes a kind of living history of the English education system. Some of the books can be traced back hundreds of years to the origins of the school" The wider educational value of what Cawthorn established has been recognised through the centuries that followed. The school library has been central to the development of the curriculum and in encouraging the wider reading that complements classroom teaching. Even in the Internet age, the school has this year recognised the continuing central importance of the library, by spending large sums in improving its structure and modernising its resources.

The links between Tonbridge and the Austen family are recognised in the school as the bi-centenary of Jane Austen's death approaches in 2017. The Reverend George Austen, Jane's father, was Cawthorn's Under Master and Usher (now known as Second Master) and plays an important role in this story. If things had worked out differently, Jane might have been brought up at Tonbridge, a precursor to Tonbridge's other famous novelist, E.M.Forster.

Martin Cawthorne is to be commended on his detailed research in telling this story of his ancestor. In the process, he shines a light on English education in the eighteenth century and on the enduring educational influence and philanthropy of the Skinners' Company. His generosity in allowing a share of the profits from the book to be given to the bursary funds will continue the tradition begun by Sir Andrew Judd and help the school to widen its access.

Tim Haynes
October 2016

PREFACE

On the 29th September 1743, at the Soho Academy in London, a schoolboy was pronounced dead from unnatural causes. James Cawthorn [1] had recently been a teacher at the school until resigning in order to take up the post of Headmaster of Tonbridge School.

Almost twenty years later in April 1761, after Cawthorn's untimely death from a riding accident, a schoolboy was apparently found dead at Tonbridge School after having been locked in a cupboard by the headmaster and forgotten. According to "the school's favourite ghost story" [2], a remorseful Cawthorn still haunts the school to this day.

Apart from the fact that James Cawthorn had only recently departed the scene of both of these deaths, there are no similarities between them whatsoever.

INTRODUCTION

In historical accounts of Tonbridge School, James Cawthorn is usually depicted as a strict disciplinarian with an almost despotic approach as headmaster. Boys under his charge are described in turn as being either terrified of him, humiliated by him or, in the case of one poor soul, locked in a cupboard, forgotten and left to starve to death. He does, however, act as master and mentor to some of the school's most prominent Old Boys; notably George Austen, father of the novelist Jane Austen, who after graduating from Oxford returns to Tonbridge in order to become Cawthorn's deputy.

Cawthorn's dedication to the school is also such that, during his tenure as headmaster, the school gets its first purpose-built library which appears in part to have been funded from the head's own pocket. The establishment of the library was a joint undertaking involving James Cawthorn, George Austen and the Worshipful Company of Skinners who govern the school. The development was not however without controversy and the unfortunate death of a schoolboy played a significant part in the saga. George Austen's involvement also helped to shape the future course of his life and led to him leaving Tonbridge, the town of his birth.

This book investigates the available historical evidence in order to uncover the story of how the first library building at Tonbridge came to be built and to establish the truth behind the myths surrounding one of the school's most controversial and enigmatic headmasters. In doing so, it also shines a light on the formative years of the life of George Austen, father of one of Britain's most much-loved novelists.

CHAPTER ONE

The Death of a Schoolboy

Nineteen-year-old Thomas Ricketts died whilst a pupil at the Soho Academy in 1743. He was killed by a single stab wound to the stomach after an argument with another schoolboy at the Academy, fifteen-year-old William Chetwynd. The wound was inflicted on the 26th September 1743 and Ricketts died three days later. The details of Thomas Ricketts' death were established in October 1743 when Chetwynd stood trial at the Old Bailey [1].

According to the transcripts of the court case, Chetwynd had shared a piece of Simnel cake with Ricketts but when Ricketts had asked for more, he had refused to give him any. Not willing to take no for an answer, the young Ricketts had reached past Chetwynd and grabbed a piece of the cake, which Chetwynd had just cut for himself. Chetwynd responded by jabbing at Ricketts with the knife he had used to cut the cake and, unfortunately, pierced the boy's abdomen just below his navel. These facts were established after a number of witnesses present at the time were cross-examined and are most clearly described by the evidence given by a maid at the school, Hannah Humphreys, who saw what had happened:

> "I was then from the Bureau about three yards, and Mr Ricketts came up to me, and said, Hannah, I have got some Cake (I had a Stocking in my Hand which I was darning). Upon, Mr Ricketts saying he had got some Cake, Mr Chetwynd came from his Bureau, to my Right-Hand, and in a very short Time Mr Ricketts said, Hannah, Mr Chetwynd has stabbed me" [2].

Once the facts of the incident had been established, a number of other parties were called to give evidence as the Court investigated the chain of events after the stabbing. These witnesses included the proprietor and headmaster of the academy, Martin Clare, who had rather belatedly realised the seriousness of the wound and only called for medical assistance the following morning. The doctors who attended to Ricketts were also cross-examined and confirmed that,

> "… the wound was the Occasion of his death" [3].

With all of the evidence having been heard, a detailed and lengthy legal argument ensued between the counsel for the prosecution and that for the defence, as the Court grappled with the question of whether or not Chetwynd should be tried for manslaughter, or the more serious charge of murder. In the end the Court was unable to agree and the case was referred to a higher authority consisting of a panel of twelve judges who had the authority to decide what charge the defendant should face and could also pass sentence by way of a "special verdict".

Martin Clare's Soho Academy

Thomas Ricketts' death was a profoundly personal tragedy for the families of both the boys involved in the altercation at the Soho Academy. It was also deeply troubling for the school and its headmaster Martin Clare, who had founded the Academy in around 1719.

Clare was an exceptionally energetic and well-connected eighteenth century educationalist and in the few short decades leading up to the death of Ricketts in 1743 had set the Soho Academy on course to become a "famous institution of the eighteenth century"[4]. The Academy was vocational in nature, with a stated intention of preparing young men to be "fitted for business"[5]. Although, as Clare makes clear in the introduction to a textbook he first publishes in 1720 – *Youth's Introduction to Trade and Business, for the use of schools* [6], the eighteenth century businessman needed a liberal education as a basis for his vocational training. As such, the subjects covered at the Academy, listed in Clare's order of preference, included Latin, English, French, Writing, Arithmetic, Bookkeeping, Drawing, Geography, Mathematics, Geometry, Astronomy, Experimental and Natural Philosophy, and Algebra.

Clare was a close friend of the French Huguenot Dr John Theophilus Desaguliers, whom he credits with assisting him in writing another of his books, *Motion of Fluids* [7], first published in 1735. Desaguliers, in turn, is closely associated with Benjamin Worster who ran a rival London academy "The Little Tower Street Academy" just off Soho Square which often encountered strong opposition from the High Church authorities for its scientific and experimental interpretation of the world. These were both schools that were very much in the vanguard of the "Enlightenment". Like Desaguliers, Clare was a prominent member of the Freemasons, where he was appointed a Grand Steward in 1735 at the same ceremony at which William Hogarth was also appointed Grand Steward. Also, like Desaguliers, he was well known for giving educational lectures. In Clare's case, these lectures were most often at meetings of the King's Arms Masonic Lodge rather than the more public lectures delivered by his friend and editor. Clare's forcefulness in promoting both himself and his Academy was not always appreciated as is evidenced by a handwritten note on the flyleaf of *Motion of Fluids* in the British Library referring to Clare's application to become a Fellow of the Royal Society, which observes that when,

"… standing candidate for election into the Royal Society, it was objected that he sought that title to give a sanction to his profession of instructing Youth and to his productions; whereupon he declared that he would not make any public use of the said title" [8].

Despite the objection he was duly elected as FRS in 1735.

The death of a boy whilst in the care of an educational

institution was a noteworthy event and Thomas Ricketts' death and the subsequent Old Bailey trial of William Chetwynd were widely reported in the newspapers of the day. Articles appeared in popular and learned periodicals. The *Gentleman's Magazine*, a monthly publication with a national circulation, covered the case[9] and it also appeared in the *London Magazine* with the original court case reported in the October 1743 [10] edition and further articles appearing in both December 1743 [11] and January 1744 [12]. A number of regional titles also carried the story.

The case featured as one of the earliest published in the somewhat more tabloid *Newgate Chronicles*, a series of flysheets covering particularly lurid or topical court cases of the day which were printed and then sold in the streets for a penny each. Thomas Ricketts' death and the subsequent trial of William Chetwynd appeared under the title:

"A curious case of a schoolboy who killed another boy during a quarrel about a cake… " [13]

Thomas Ricketts' death, the Old Bailey Court case and the ensuing coverage in the press of the day were a serious setback for the Soho Academy and its proprietor Martin Clare. An educational institution lacking basic disciplinary boundaries and where boys in the school's care killed each other with knives was not the type of school Clare had so assiduously promoted since its formation. Although it survived and went on to prosper, the death of Thomas Ricketts was a defining moment in the Academy's history.

Guilty by association

It was not only the Soho Academy that would suffer the consequences of Thomas Ricketts' death. Working at the Academy in 1743 was a young teacher called James Cawthorn. Originally from Yorkshire, James was the son of Thomas Cawthorn, an entrepreneurial Yeoman who had a number of business interests in and around the city of Sheffield including a bookshop which the young James had looked after whilst his father attended to his other interests.

Prior to matriculating at Cambridge University, Cawthorn had harboured thoughts of becoming a poet and had a number of poems published including one in the *Gentleman's Magazine* in 1735 [14]. Cawthorn failed to complete his studies at Cambridge and there is no evidence of him actually graduating. Instead he moved to London where he may have hoped to further his literary career. How he came to be employed at Martin Clare's Soho Academy is unclear but it could have been as a result of a business connection of his father's. Thomas Cawthorn had a mutual business associate of one of London's most prominent printers, Henry Woodfall, who was an active publisher in London political circles at this time and was well known to the Speaker of the House of Commons, the Right Hon Arthur Onslow MP. Martin Clare was tutor to the Speaker's son, George Onslow, to whom he dedicated the 5th edition of *Youth's Introduction to Trade and Business* published in 1740 [15]. Henry Woodfall and Arthur Onslow would later be neighbours when each lived in apartments in Cannonbury House, Middlesex [16].

Whatever the means by which Cawthorn became an

employee of Clare's, he was very soon a member of the family at the Academy; in a quite literal sense when he married Martin Clare's daughter Mary on the 14th November 1742 [17]. This was a momentous year for Cawthorn as prior to his marriage to Mary he had taken holy orders and was ordained as a priest at St Margaret's Church, Westminster on the 9th September 1742[18], on the authority of the Archbishop of Canterbury Dr John Potter. Mary was, however, a young lady with a delicate constitution and the London air did not appear to suit her particularly well. It was very fortuitous for the newlyweds therefore when, less than a year after their marriage, a vacancy arose for a headmaster at Tonbridge School in Kent.

In the summer of 1743 the Rev. Richard Spencer had been Headmaster of Tonbridge for twenty-eight years and both he and the Worshipful Company of Skinners, who governed the school, were of the opinion that he had been in the post for long enough. His predecessor, the Rev. Thomas Roots, had been headmaster for forty-six years and towards the end of his tenure had become such a liability that the number of boys at the school had dwindled away to barely a handful. At the time of his appointment, Spencer had very quickly set to work on turning the school around and within a decade the number of boys at the school had risen to over eighty. They remained at a high level for the next ten years but after that, as the headmaster appeared to lose his earlier enthusiasm numbers began to fall once more so that by the summer of 1743 there were only forty-four boys on the register. It must therefore have come as something of a relief to the Governors when at a Skinners' Court of Assistants meeting on the 26th April 1743[19] Spencer offered his resignation.

Richard Spencer's resignation was accepted at the following Court of Assistants meeting held on the 2nd June 1743 [20], when it was also resolved to start a search for a new headmaster. It was agreed that enquiries were to be made for suitable candidates.

It is difficult to believe that James Cawthorn would have been one of the candidates approached by the Skinners. He was only twenty-four years old, had limited teaching experience and had not previously been the headmaster of a school. What is more likely is that Cawthorn heard about the vacancy and in turn approached the Skinners. There are a number of ways in which he could have heard the news, with his father-in-law, Martin Clare, being the most obvious likely source of information given his wide-ranging network of contacts.

London Literary Circles

However, a more intriguing possibility also presents itself. Cawthorn was known to the bookselling and publishing community in London and was familiar with the bookshops around Paternoster Row and St Paul's Cathedral. He developed a close, life-long friendship with a bookseller called Charles Hitch, whose shop, and its location in the heart of the booksellers' district, he refers to in one of his poems, in which a learned and academic character,

> "… would sometimes drop his gown
> And take a winter jaunt to town;
> Often called in at Hitch's shop
> And Dined at Dolly's on a chop" [21]

The "Dolly's" referred to is Dolly's Chop House in Queen's Head Court, Paternoster Row, which was a short walk from Hitch's shop and was popular with both booksellers and a wider literary clientele including the likes of Swift, Fielding and Pope. It also catered for the not insubstantial appetite of the composer George Frederic Handel whose agent, John Christopher Smith, sent his son, also called John Christopher, to be educated at Martin Clare's Soho Academy where the fees were paid for by Handel [22].

Charles Hitch was one of the most prominent publishers of his day and had been apprenticed to Arthur Bettesworth whose daughter he had married. At the time that Cawthorn was working in London, Hitch was in a loose publishing partnership, called a "conger"[23] with a number of other important publishers including the "eminent bookseller" [24] Stephen Austen, whose shop was a short walk from Paternoster Row. Hitch and Austen published a number of books together, for example, in 1739 *The Travels and Adventures of Edward Brown, Esq. Formerly a Merchant of London,* printed by J. Applebee for A. Bettesworth and C. Hitch in Paternoster Row; William Hinchliffe at Dryden's Head under the Piazza of the Royal Exchange; and Stephen Austen at the Angel and Bible in St Paul's Churchyard [25]. Stephen Austen knew Tonbridge School very well. He had been born in Tonbridge in 1704, the sixth son of John Austen's seven children. His father, however, had died when he was only an infant and his mother, Elizabeth Weller, had taken a job as housekeeper to the headmaster of the nearby Sevenoaks School in order to ensure her sons all received a sound education.

On completion of his studies, Stephen Austen was

apprenticed to the publisher William Innys [26] who operated from a shop in St Paul's Churchyard. This shop was popular with the Masters of the Soho Academy's rival educational institution, the Little Tower Street Academy; Thomas Watts and Benjamin Worster [27] who, like their colleague Desaguliers, gave public lectures in addition to lecturing at their Academy. However, whilst their fellow teacher, and Martin Clare's editor for *Motion of Fluids*, Dr Desaguliers, was lecturing at the Bedford Coffee House in Covent Garden, which was popular with Freemasons and members of the Royal Society [28], Watts and Worster lectured in William Innys' bookshop. Innys was one of a long list of publishers, which also included the partnership of Arthur Bettesworth and Charles Hitch, who in 1731 published *Philosophical Transactions*, the journal of the Royal Society [29]. On the death of Arthur Bettesworth, William Innys continued to publish books with Charles Hitch, such as *Boerhaave's Aphorisms: concerning the Knowledge and care of Diseases,* printed by W. Innys at the West End of St Paul's and C. Hitch in Paternoster Row, 1742[30]. In 1744 Charles Hitch and Stephen Austen were collaborating in the publication of the 2nd edition of *Modern History of the present state of all nations* by Thomas Salmon, printed for T. Longman in Paternoster Row, T. Osborne in Gray's Inn; J Shuckburgh in Fleet St; C. Hitch in Paternoster Row; S. Austen in Newgate St and J. Rivington in St Paul's Churchyard[31]. Whereas in 1745 Innys again collaborated with Hitch in a publication in which Henry Woodfall also had an interest, *A Course of Experimental Philosophy* by Desaguliers, printed by W. Innys; T. Longman and T. Shewell; and C. Hitch in Paternoster Row and M. Senex in Fleet Street and *The ornaments are those used by Henry Woodfall* [32]. Historical evidence also suggests that Austen, Hitch and Innys were all elected to serve as Common Councilmen of the Castle Baynard district of London from the 7th January 1740[33]. James Cawthorn and Stephen Austen clearly moved in the same London literary circles.

Stephen Austen and Tonbridge

Stephen Austen also knew Richard Spencer, Headmaster of Tonbridge School and when Spencer started a subscription roll to raise funds to buy books for the school, Stephen Austen's name appears as a donor in 1729 [34].

At the time that Cawthorn was in London working as a teacher at the Soho Academy, Austen had a more immediate link to Tonbridge School. His brother William had trained as a surgeon and had settled in Tonbridge, where he married a local girl Rebecca Walter, the widow of a local physician William Walter. The couple had three children who survived beyond infancy but Rebecca unfortunately died whilst the children were still young. William remarried Susanna Kelk, also of Tonbridge, but in 1737, a few years after his second marriage, he also died and his widow made it clear that she had no interest in bringing up her stepchildren. Consequently, William's young son George, and two daughters Philadelphia and Leonora were sent initially to live with their uncle in London. Stephen Austen is usually portrayed as adopting a cold and uncaring attitude to the three young charges suddenly thrust into his care,

> "... Uncle Stephen had not taken kindly to receiving these three infant charges into his home... How well George remembered the day when he and his sisters presented themselves at their uncle's door, to be received 'with neglect, if not with positive unkindness'" [35].

This does, however, seem a little harsh given Stephen's circumstances at the time. Despite his own very unpromising start in life he had completed his apprenticeship with William Innys and set up in business on his own account. He was steadily establishing himself as a bookseller of some repute and had started to take on apprentices of his own. He had also married and his wife had given birth to a son who was still a young boy of only five years old at the time his brother's abandoned children arrived on the doorstep of what, by that time, would have been an already-crowded little home above the shop. The last thing that Stephen Austen needed at this point in his life was more hungry mouths to feed. The eldest child, Philadelphia, appears to have been moved on to live with other distant relatives before being apprenticed to a milliner in 1745[36]. Leonora and George Austen, however, were provided with a home in Stephen's bookshop until George was sent back to Tonbridge to live with his aunt Elizabeth Hooper sometime between May 1740 and the 12th May 1741[37]. This was two years before Richard Spencer's resignation and George Austen was enrolled as a day boy at Tonbridge School. His cousin Henry Austen was Head Boy of the school at this time.

James Cawthorn and Stephen Austen would quite likely

have known each other during the time that Cawthorn worked at the Soho Academy, given the overlapping social and literary circles in which they both moved. Cawthorn may well have also met George Austen during this time if, for example, Austen had been left "minding the bookshop" for his uncle in the same way in which the young James Cawthorn had looked after the family bookshop whilst his father attended to other business interests. The Austen family was well connected to Tonbridge School and so it is not unreasonable to suppose that it may have been from Stephen Austen that James Cawthorn heard about the vacancy for a headmaster at the school in the summer of 1743.

A New Headmaster for Tonbridge School

Whatever the means by which Cawthorn heard of the vacancy at Tonbridge School he nevertheless put himself forward for the position. This is documented in the Skinners' Court Records where in the first instance at a Court of Assistants meeting on the 24th July 1743 the Skinners decided that,

> "… the Election of a Master for Tunbridge School be on… the fourth day of August and that in the meantime Mr Russell (Skinners' Company Secretary) do write letters to the several candidates to inform them thereof… " [38]

In order to ensure a good turnout of members on the 4th August, it was also ordered,

> "... that notice be inserted at the bottom of the summons which shall be delivered to the respective members of the Court of Assistants that the election will be on that day" [39].

The summons to members certainly had the desired effect, for at the Court of Assistants meeting held on the 4th August 1743 a long list of Skinners attending the meeting is noted in the court records. Unfortunately, the letters to prospective candidates did not appear to have the same effect, for only two candidates presented themselves to petition for the vacant headmaster's position and to offer testimonials in support of their petitions. One was James Cawthorn and the other, the Rev. Gilbert Stephens, a clergyman from Oxford who was older than Cawthorn and had experience in preparing boys for entry into Oxford University. It was clearly a straight fight between youth and enthusiasm on the one hand and age and experience on the other.

The two candidates were in turn interviewed by the members of the Skinners' Court and their testimonials considered. Despite the fact that only Cawthorn and Stephens had shown interest in the position of Headmaster of Tonbridge School, left vacant by Richard Spencer's resignation, the minutes of the meeting illustrate that the Skinners were clearly impressed with the qualities of both candidates. Unfortunately, only one could prevail and be appointed to the role of headmaster, and at the end of the meeting the Skinners' records, whilst making no mention of the somewhat disappointing response to the search for a new head, are very clear on the choice of who would replace the Rev. Richard Spencer as Headmaster of Tonbridge School,

> "... the terms and conditions therein mentioned were severally read which said Office or place of Schoolmaster was conferred upon the Rev. Gilbert Stephens. To hold the same from the resignation of the said Mr Richard Spencer according to the Will and Statutes of Sir Andrew Judd and the pleasure of this Company" [40].

Age and experience had clearly triumphed over youth and enthusiasm.

James Cawthorn must have been bitterly disappointed at this outcome and, as this was still over a month before the death of Thomas Ricketts, it is clear that at this time the unfortunate events surrounding Ricketts' death were not to blame for Cawthorn's failure to obtain the appointment of Headmaster of Tonbridge School.

Fate, however, had still to play a part.

Fate Lends a Hand

Six weeks after the election of the Rev. Gilbert Stephens, a routine committee meeting was taking place at Skinners' Hall in which the Livery Company's property holdings were being subjected to a regular review. The Court of Lease's meeting held on the 16th September 1743 was, however, interrupted by an unexpected visitor as is made clear in the court minutes.

> "The Rev. Mr Gilbert Stephens who was at the last Court chosen to succeed the Rev. Mr Richard Spencer as Schoolmaster of this Company's School at Tunbridge having heard that this committee was sitting, came therein… " [41]

Stephens addressed the committee and opened proceedings with effusive thanks for his earlier appointment for which,

> "… he was highly sensible of the great favour the Company had done him in conferring the said Office upon him and for which he should ever retain the most grateful remembrance" [42].

Before moving on to the real purpose of his request to speak to the committee when he dropped the following bombshell in announcing,

> "… that an offer having been very lately made him of something which he apprehended would be more to his ease and satisfaction as well as advantage. He therefore chose to resign the same and hoped that the Company would be pleased to elect some other person in his stead" [43].

The immediate reaction of the committee members present on the 16th September to this utterly unexpected news is not recorded. However, the confusion into which the Skinners were thrown by Stephens' announcement, so close to the date at which he was to take up his appointment, is nevertheless clear from the final entry in the minutes,

> "Whereupon this committee informed him they would desire the Master to call a Court for that purpose on two (sic) days next the 20th in September"[44].

A full Court of Assistants meeting was duly held four (sic) days later on the 20th September [45] when a letter from Stephens confirming his resignation was read out. The Skinners then discussed what options they had available to them and the sense of frustration and near panic is palpable as they needed to find a replacement for Spencer but had only days in which to make a decision. A further meeting was called for the 27th September 1743 at which the Skinners recognise they will need to decide what they are going to do and will also have to inform Richard Spencer about their decisions relating to his chosen successor.

Another New Headmaster for Tonbridge School

The Worshipful Company of Skinners' Court of Assistants meeting held on the 27th September 1743 took place the day after Thomas Ricketts was stabbed and was the same day on which Martin Clare, having belatedly recognised the seriousness of his wound, called for a doctor.

The Skinners' Company would have been completely unaware of the events unfolding at the Soho Academy as they set about undertaking the business of finding a replacement for the unreliable Gilbert Stephens. Their deliberations are recorded in the court minutes for the day when proceedings were opened with,

> "… the Petition and Testimonials of the Rev. James Cawthorne, Clerk were read for the Office or place of Schoolmaster of this Company's School at Tunbridge" [46].

It is not clear if James Cawthorn knew anything about Thomas Ricketts' stabbing or the seriousness of his condition at the time at which the Skinners were once again discussing his petition for the role of Headmaster of Tonbridge School. However, if he did know anything he may well have chosen to remain silent on the matter, particularly as it is clear from the court minutes that his suitability for the role was being questioned anyway given his youth and limited teaching experience. Although the Skinners had been impressed with Cawthorn when he had originally petitioned them in competition with Stephens, they were nevertheless acutely aware of the risk they would be taking by appointing such a young and relatively inexperienced headmaster. Cawthorn may have been qualified to do the job but that did not necessarily mean that he was a suitable candidate. The Skinners, however, were in a difficult position. The new academic year was almost upon them and, having accepted the resignation of the incumbent Richard Spencer, they were under pressure to find a replacement. The response to the original search had hardly been overwhelming and it now appeared that

James Cawthorn was their only remaining option unless they wished to try and retain Spencer's services for another year. When the Skinners did eventually make a decision it was only after lengthy consultation and deliberation as is shown in the Court minutes:

> "Whereupon, this Court after reading the Will and Statutes of Sir Andrew Judd, and it appearing that the said Mr Cawthorne was every way qualified did confer the said place of Schoolmaster of their free school at Tunbridge upon him" [47].

Despite their reservations the Skinners had decided that Cawthorn was capable of doing the job and in the absence of any viable and attractive alternatives they most likely felt that it was at least worth giving him a chance. The urgency of the appointment is clear in the next sentence:

> "To hold the same from Michaelmas Day next according to the Will and Statutes of Sir Andrew Judd and the pleasure of this Company" [48].

Michaelmas Day was the 29th September which therefore gave Cawthorn only two days from the date of the meeting of the Court of Assistants confirming his appointment, to get down to Tonbridge and take over the school. The Secretary of the Skinners, Mr Russell, was instructed to,

> "… acquaint the Rev. Mr Richard Spencer that this Company have made choice of the Rev. Mr James Cawthorne to succeed him as Schoolmaster

of Tunbridge School. To hold the same from Michaelmas Day next and to desire the said Mr Spencer to deliver the position thereof to him" [49].

The resulting letter to Richard Spencer to such effect most probably accompanied James Cawthorn on his journey to Tonbridge to take up his appointment; such was the urgency of the situation.

So it was that on the 29th September 1743, the Rev. Mr James Cawthorn arrived in Tonbridge to take over as Headmaster of Tonbridge School. This was the same day on which Thomas Ricketts was declared dead from a stab wound at Cawthorn's previous school, the Soho Academy in London.

The Storm Breaks

James Cawthorn was not in any way implicated in the death of Thomas Ricketts; he was not identified as having been present at the altercation between Ricketts and Chetwynd and was not called as either a defendant or indeed a witness at the subsequent Old Bailey trial. It is nevertheless difficult to think of a more inauspicious start to his tenure as Headmaster of Tonbridge School and the reaction of the Skinners as the subsequent news stories unfolded in the press can only be imagined.

To be fair, the reporting of the Old Bailey court case by the learned periodicals, the *Gentleman's Magazine* and the *London Magazine*, were restrained and factual with both publications restricting their reports to identifying the names of the individuals involved in the case. Chetwynd and Ricketts were nevertheless identified as schoolboys and the fact that Chetwynd was on trial, charged with the murder of Ricketts by stabbing him to death was covered. Quite when the first copies of the *Newgate Chronicle's* "Curious case of the Schoolboy who killed another boy…" was sold on the street is unclear, but although it too gave a reasonably balanced account of the trial, the language used was somewhat more colourful. Extracts of the prosecution's case against Chetwynd were detailed such that:

> "Mr Rickets was stabbed, having no weapon drawn in his hand, and not having before struck the person who stabbed him" [50].

Readers were also left in no doubt as to where the alleged schoolboy murder took place for when describing the defendant, William Chetwynd, it is explained that:

> "This unfortunate young gentleman was placed at the academy in Soho Square… " [51]

This was, of course, the very same academy at which the new Headmaster of Tonbridge School had until recently been employed as a teacher, indeed, at the time that Ricketts was stabbed.

Although the reaction of the Skinners to the unfolding news about the killing of a schoolboy at the Soho Academy is not recorded, the reaction of parents of boys at Tonbridge School to the – already controversial –

appointment of James Cawthorn was clear and brutal. The numbers on the school register, which had been falling steadily for most of the past decade of Spencer's tenure, now plummeted, dropping from the forty-four registered in May 1743 to only twenty-six by May of 1744[52]. Families voted with their feet.

James Cawthorn and the Curious Case of the Schoolboy who was killed

James Cawthorn did not have anything to do with the death of Thomas Ricketts. Nevertheless, the curious death of the schoolboy who was killed after an argument over a piece of cake, cast an unwelcome shadow over his appointment as Headmaster of Tonbridge School. He could perhaps take some comfort from the fact that not all families chose to withdraw their boys, including the Austen family where young George Austen remained at Tonbridge after his cousin Henry moved to Cambridge University when he matriculated at Queens' College for the Michaelmas term, 1743. This may have been because it was indeed through the Austen family that Cawthorn had found out about the vacancy and been encouraged to put his name forward. A more likely explanation, however, is that George was simply given no choice; he had nowhere else to go.

CHAPTER TWO

Reports of another Curious Death

The death of Thomas Ricketts undoubtedly overshadowed the start of James Cawthorn's tenure as Headmaster of Tonbridge School. He is, however, more usually remembered in histories of the school for the subsequent death of a schoolboy at the end of his career.

Reports of a Curious Death at Tonbridge School

Septimus Rivington is the first to allude to the possibility of a skeleton in the late headmaster's cupboard when in *The History of Tonbridge School from Its Foundation in 1553 to the Present Date*, first published in 1869, he explains that:

> Mr Cawthorn was out for a ride, and while his horse was preparing to drink at the pond… on Quarry Hill, Tonbridge, it stumbled and threw its rider. This caused Mr Cawthorn an injury of a broken leg, which, in a few days after, April 15, proved fatal to him. A tradition since that time has

been handed down in the School that the ghost of the stern master perambulated the dormitories of the old building at midnight on April 15, with clanking chain and measured step. [1]

In 1947 D. C. Somervell in *A History of Tonbridge School* adds a little flesh to the bones of the story:

James Cawthorn was a Yorkshireman and left the reputation of a severe disciplinarian, so severe that his ghost remorsefully haunted the school house dormitories for more than a hundred years … Cawthorn locked a boy up in an attic as a punishment and then forgot all about him. After an unspecified interval of time he recollected the unfortunate youth while out riding, started to gallop home, fell and broke his leg. The boy was subsequently found in the attic starved to death. [2]

Rivington and Somervell had set the tone and successive historians of the school followed their lead. So much so, that by the late twentieth century, histories of the school had firmly positioned Cawthorn as something of a caricature of "a blunt Yorkshireman" [3] and, moreover, one with a "reputation for severity, in the mould of Keate of Eton and Busby of Westminster" [4]. Such was Cawthorn's reputation, that by 1991 Barry Orchard in *A Look at the Head and the Fifty*, had moved on from merely repeating the previous accounts of Cawthorn's alleged misdemeanour, to also contemplating the possible consequences of his apparent criminal act:

> In 1761 Cawthorn died from a riding accident, aged 41. He stopped on Quarry Hill to let his horse drink from a trough, fell off and broke his leg. He died a few days later. The story is that the accident happened as he was hurrying back to school to release a boy whom he had locked in a cupboard and forgotten. The boy was found dead, and, if he himself had not died, Cawthorn must have been charged with manslaughter. [5]

So it was that a little over a hundred years after his death, historians of Tonbridge School had linked Cawthorn's name to the curious death of a schoolboy who was killed whilst in the care of the headmaster. The stories were repeated and embellished over the subsequent 150 years so that within a quarter of a millennium James Cawthorn was firmly established as the pantomime villain of Tonbridge School Headmasters. Maids had to be employed to sit with terrified boarders on the anniversary of Cawthorn's death to protect the poor innocents from the attentions of his tormented ghost [6], and as Septimus Rivington explained,

> "… any boy will tell you who Mr Cawthorne was, whilst all the other Head Masters are almost a dead letter to them" [7].

The reality of what happened at the time of James Cawthorn's death as presented by the historical evidence of the time is, needless to say, somewhat less colourful.

The Historical Reality

On Thursday 16th April 1761 a Special Court of Assistants meeting was convened at Skinners' Hall, chaired by the Master of the Skinners' Company, Mr Henry Kent. The reason for the meeting is recorded in the Skinners' Court Records:

> "At this Court a letter from Miss Cawthorne, sister of the Rev. Mr Cawthorne, Master of Tunbridge School directed to Mr Gregg the Clerk of this Company acquainting him with the death of the said Mr Cawthorne was read…" [8]

On Saturday 18th April 1761, the following article appeared on the front page of the *London Chronicle*:

> "On Wednesday last died the Rev. Mr Cawthorne, Master of the Free Grammar School at Tunbridge. A gentleman of extensive learning and good natural abilities, indefatigable in his profession, of an obliging and cheerful disposition and very much esteemed and beloved by all his acquaintance. His death, which is indeed a public loss, was occasioned by a violent fall from his horse" [9].

These notices are important as much for what they do not say as for their actual content. There are no references whatsoever to any discovery of a dead schoolboy found at the school. Neither do any subsequent news articles appear to such effect. In fact, the only references to Cawthorn's death in the days immediately after his accident and indeed subsequently are couched in similarly reverential terms. No court cases are convened and no newspaper articles appear covering the death of a boy at Tonbridge School during this time.

Cawthorn was buried in the parish church in Tonbridge where his sister Elizabeth commissioned a marble monument carved with a glowing eulogy to her brother's memory. It is highly unlikely that the church or the Skinners' Company would have sanctioned such a move if there was even the slightest grain of truth in the lurid stories about the poor unfortunate boy who supposedly died at the headmaster's hands.

The reason for the complete lack of any historical evidence in relation to the schoolboy who died at the hands of Cawthorn at the end of his tenure as Headmaster of Tonbridge School is obviously very clear. There was no schoolboy who died. The story is a complete figment of an over active schoolboy imagination and as Somervell goes on to explain:

> "The only element of truth in the story is that Cawthorn did in fact die as the result of a fall from his horse" [10].

The Reasons behind the Myth

It seems inconceivable that James Cawthorn's name should be linked to the death of Thomas Ricketts and that his remorseful ghost should haunt Tonbridge School years later for an incident in which the late headmaster was not in any way involved. Indeed, an incident that had occurred at the Soho Academy in London rather than at Tonbridge School. There is also no historical evidence whatsoever to link Cawthorn's name to the subsequent death of any boy at Tonbridge School at the end of his tenure as headmaster. Instead, in order to understand the reasons why the myths surrounding the Rev. James Cawthorn appear to be so far removed from the historical reality it is necessary to look elsewhere.

In this regard, it is necessary to look no further than the headmaster's greatest legacy to Tonbridge School – The Cawthorn Library.

CHAPTER THREE

Building Foundations

Throughout the course of the eighteenth century printing technology steadily improved, and as a result, books became cheaper to print and consequently more readily available. Over time this meant that whereas previously only the rich colleges of Oxford and Cambridge, and schools attached to major theological institutions such as Westminster and Winchester, had the means to afford libraries, they now became more common. Schools which had previously relied upon donations of books from generous benefactors or which raised funds to buy books by way of a modest levy on their pupils, found themselves accumulating collections at an accelerating rate. This was quite simply a function of there being more books in circulation and them being less expensive items to collect. This more rapid accumulation of books soon made it desirable for schools to start building separate rooms in order to house their growing libraries. Eton College opened a purpose-built library designed by Thomas Rowland between the years 1725 and 1729[1]. Rowlands Library was capable of housing 20,000 volumes despite the school actually owning less than 5,000 books at the time the building was commissioned. This was because schools had quickly discovered that the establishment of a separate library building often had the effect of increasing the number of books donated by benefactors. In 1736 Richard Topham duly donated hundreds of books to Eton, together with his famous collection of prints, drawings and watercolours of classical antiquities which significantly enhanced the scope of the library[2]. A purpose-built library became an increasingly important necessity for any school which wished to establish itself as a destination academic institution.

A Library for Tonbridge School

Tonbridge School was founded in 1553 and, like the Soho Academy founded 150 years later, the driving force behind the establishment of the school was a single individual. However, whereas the Soho Academy was the creation of a notable educationalist Martin Clare, who ran his school as a private business, Tonbridge was founded by a man who did not have a background in education and the school was never intended to be a business venture established to enrich its founder. Sir Andrew Judd was a very successful merchant and a member of the Worshipful Company of Skinners, a Livery Company originally founded to protect and promote the interests of merchants dealing in the preparation and trading of furs. He was also a notable philanthropist, and towards the end of his life he established a school in the town of his birth, Tonbridge. He endowed the school with property in London, the rents from which would help to support the running costs of the school. From its inception, Tonbridge was intended as a school which would educate a mixture of local day boys from in and around the town, sometimes called irregulars, and boarders from further afield who were often, but not exclusively, connected to the Skinners' Company. On his death, the founding statutes, drawn up by Sir Andrew, stipulated that the school would come under the care and governance of the Worshipful Company of Skinners, thus establishing what has since developed into a long tradition of involvement in education by the Livery Company.

The Founder's Statutes for Tonbridge School also provided that each boy on admission to the school would pay sixpence towards books "to remain in the Scholle for the common use of the Schollers"[3]. The modest collection of books which this levy was capable of funding was supplemented in 1620 by the "bounteous minds"[4] of some generous benefactors who were encouraged to follow the example of Sir Thomas Smythe, grandson of Sir Andrew Judd, founder of the school and "endow the free school with their gifts"[5]. These gifts included the donation of a number of dictionaries, and an inventory of school property made in 1640 records a library collection of some fifty-four assorted volumes [6]. By 1680 a more detailed catalogue of the school's books records that the number held had risen to ninety-six [7], although unfortunately, "to their great injury"[8], the books were stored in the schoolroom. This was despite a number of headmasters, including the noted 17th century educationalist Christopher Wase, who was headmaster between 1662 and 1668, recognising the need for grammar schools to have a separate "room for books" [9].

Cawthorn's immediate predecessor, the Rev. Richard Spencer, was successful in persuading the Governors to spend the money saved by not employing a deputy, known as an Usher, when school numbers had been low, on building eight bookcases. These stood at the end of the schoolroom for many years, providing a home for the school's still-modest collection of books. He also started a Library Subscription Roll [10] as a means of raising funds for the purchase of new books for the school. The funds raised in this way could be added to the sixpence each boy had to pay into the Common Box upon entry into the school, money which was also available to buy books. A catalogue commissioned by the Skinners on Spencer's resignation records that by 1743 the number of books held at the school had risen to 636 [11]. These were, however, still kept in the schoolroom on the bookcases built during Spencer's tenure.

Spencer was in many ways an energetic and imaginative headmaster and would often find a way of forcing the hand of the Skinners to provide the funds he felt were necessary to develop the school. Quite apart from his efforts to develop a library at Tonbridge, there are a number of instances recorded in the court records where Spencer finds himself in trouble for spending money on necessary repairs at the school before he has received permission to do so. Like his predecessors before him, however, he was singularly unable to persuade the Skinners' Company to construct a purpose-built library at Tonbridge School. The reason for the Skinners' reluctance to embark on such an ambitious course was quite simply down to a lack of available funds. Much of the property in

London which had been left in trust by Sir Andrew Judd to support the school had been destroyed in the Great Fire and the associated rent roll had not sufficiently recovered. The fluctuating fortunes of the school under successive headmasters had also resulted in a highly unstable register of boys, with all the attendant uncertainty in respect of the school's fee income.

Towards the end of his term as headmaster, Spencer seems to have become disillusioned and school numbers once again started to decline. Parents at the school were also increasingly expressing their disquiet about the quality of the education being provided. For example, in the summer of 1743, when one boy was removed from the school, his guardian was uncompromising in explaining the reasons why:

> "I have taken Mr Lade from Tonbridge School where he was placed by his Uncle, and where he has been about 4 years, and where if he had stayed any longer he would have forgotten even to read which he doth now… indifferently" [12].

Meanwhile, the increasingly pressing question of how to provide a separate school library building at Tonbridge remained unresolved.

James Cawthorn becomes Headmaster

It was against this background that James Cawthorn took over as headmaster on Spencer's resignation. Despite the initial further fall in the number of boys on the roll caused by his somewhat controversial appointment, he nevertheless very quickly started to stamp his authority on the school. Like Spencer before him he was also not afraid to act unilaterally if he felt the occasion warranted action, regardless of whether he had actually received permission to do so or not. The Skinners' Court books record a number of instances where, for example, Cawthorn has sought permission for building works at the school only after he has actually commissioned the works and had them completed.

Cawthorn, however, differed from his immediate predecessors in a very important respect. Whereas the headmasters who came before him were all ultimately constrained by the Skinners' Company's willingness and ability to pay for any work at the school which they requested, this was not the case for Cawthorn. For in Cawthorn's case, he would also offer to pay for the works himself if the Skinners proved either unable or unwilling to do so. For example, at a Committee of Leases Meeting held at Skinners' Hall on the 14th February 1759 to consider a number of bills submitted by Cawthorn for repairs he has had completed at the school, the following entry appears in the Skinners' Court records:

> "A letter from the Rev. Mr Cawthorne which accompanied the aforesaid Bills was read whereby the said Mr Cawthorne offered to pay such part of the aforesaid… bill as this Company should think proper" [13].

During the course of his tenure, Cawthorn appears to have developed an increasingly proprietorial approach in his role as headmaster. This may perhaps have been as a result of him having worked for the privately owned Soho Academy where the headmaster, Martin Clare, owned the school in every sense. However, it is Cawthorn's background as the son of a self-made Yorkshire Yeoman that is the key to understanding how and why he was able to develop such an approach.

The Rev. James Cawthorn differed from his predecessors in that he possessed both the character and background to ensure that Tonbridge would get its first school library building during his tenure as headmaster. To understand this point more fully it is necessary to consider both the type of character that he was and also the background from which he came. It is a background which simultaneously shaped his character whilst also providing him with the means which enabled him to succeed where his predecessors had failed. It is these two factors when combined which resulted in Tonbridge School getting its first library building during James Cawthorn's tenure as headmaster.

In trying to understand Cawthorn's character as illustrated during his tenure as Headmaster of Tonbridge, his term of office needs to be considered during two quite distinct periods. The early period covers the years up to the mid 1750s; a decade during which Cawthorn seems to have been determined to prove himself worthy of the position to which he had been so controversially appointed. From the mid 1750s, however, Cawthorn's circumstances changed and so too did his relationship with both Tonbridge School and the Skinners' Company. The library is at the centre of the story.

Cawthorn's First Year

The first real test for Cawthorn after his appointment as headmaster came in May 1744 with the annual Skinners' Company Visitation to the school. This was an annual pilgrimage to Tonbridge undertaken by a group of senior members of the Company who would travel down to the school for a couple of days in order to review the state of the school and to test the abilities of the pupils. A specially appointed examiner would accompany the members of the Company, and the six most able pupils, as chosen by the headmaster, would be questioned and their knowledge examined in a range of subjects. A number of headmasters before Cawthorn had sometimes found themselves being censured by the Skinners as a result of the poor performance of pupils under their charge.

The seriousness with which the Skinners' Company treated the first visitation to Tonbridge since Cawthorn's controversial appointment as headmaster is evident in the court records. The report of the members who made the annual pilgrimage is usually only noted by way of a short minute in the records with the details being left to sub-committees to act on if necessary. However, in the case of the visitation made on the 7 – 8th May 1744, a substantial and detailed account is recorded in the Skinners' Court records [14].

It is noted how the Skinners travelled down from

London on the 7th May and were met in the traditional way at the school door by a scholar who welcomed them in Latin. They then retired to a local inn for the evening to recover from their journey and prepare for the following day. The morning of the 8th May started with a church service in which a number of poor inhabitants of the parish were identified as being worthy recipients of the Skinners' charity and should "receive bread and cloth to be given by Mr Cawthorne at Whitsuntide" [15]. The party then moved on to the school and after inspecting the buildings and grounds, agreed a series of repairs for which cost estimates were provided by Cawthorn. Then followed the first important aspect of the visit from Cawthorn's perspective as they went into the school, where "… the Rev. Mr Nicholas Fayting, who was desired to perform the office of Examiner on the Visitation, proceeded to examine in our presence and in the presence of several Ministers and other Gentleman there assembled, the scholars of the said school… " [16]. The Skinners were, no doubt to Cawthorn's immense relief, impressed with their first meeting with the boys under his care "… who by their ready and proper answers to the several questions proposed to them by the said Examiner did sufficiently testify to the great diligence and application as well as ability of the Schoolmaster" [17].

The visitation delegation retired back to their inn for dinner and then,

> "After dinner repaired again to the school to listen to disputations and other exercises which were performed by Richard Bathurst, George Newton,

Samuel Sedgewick, William Dalyson, George Austen and John Cooke" [18].

These were the six scholars chosen by the headmaster, and his choice of boys to face the examiner is revealing, as both Newton and Sedgewick were new to the school. Their education during their short time at Tonbridge is thus wholly attributable to the new headmaster. The thirteen-year-old George Austen was one of the youngest boys to face the examiner but Cawthorn may have already known how talented a young man he was before the two were reacquainted at Tonbridge, and his confidence in his young student's ability had clearly been reinforced during his first year as his teacher.

Whatever the reasons were for Cawthorn choosing these six scholars to face the examiner during this first and most crucial visitation for the headmaster, his faith in his charges was well placed as is clear from the court records where the visiting Skinners delegation notes that the scholars,

"Severely acquitted themselves with great reputation and credit" [19].

And as such,

"To each of whom we delivered a Silver Pen quill Gift" [20].

It is clear from the account given in the court records that the first visitation to Tonbridge after Cawthorn became headmaster was a tremendous success and any lingering reservations about his appointment were dispelled.

The early evidence of Cawthorn's character whilst at Tonbridge is that of a new headmaster who was clearly self-confident in his abilities as a teacher and this confidence was soon shared by his employers. He is also prepared to put forward requests for building works at the school that he feels are necessary. His requests for building work and repairs to be undertaken were approved and all in all he completed a very satisfactory first year at Tonbridge. The regard in which he was held by the Skinners quickly began to climb.

Building on the early success

Richard Bathurst's performance as one of the scholars examined by the Rev. Mr Fayting, the Skinners' Company examiner, was instrumental in ensuring he won a Skinners' Company scholarship to study at Oxford where he matriculated at St Edmund's Hall on the 6th June 1744 [21].

The following year was a much less pressured year for Cawthorn as he built on his early success. George Newton moved on before matriculating at Oriel College, Oxford [22] and Samuel Sedgewick matriculated on the 1st July 1745 at Cawthorn's old college: Clare Hall, Cambridge [23]. This year also saw Cawthorn's younger brother Thomas move down to London from Sheffield. He opened a hardware shop in Leadenhall Market and, with the help of his older brother, was admitted to the Freedom of the Skinners' Company [24]. Cawthorn also confidently started to promote both himself and Tonbridge School. He delivered a "sermon preached before the worshipful burgesses of Westminster, at St Margaret's church" [25] on the 18th April which was well received and subsequently published by Charles Hitch with Cawthorn described on the front cover as "Master of the Grammar School at Tunbridge, Kent". There is also some evidence to suggest that for the 1745 visitation in early May, Cawthorn again chose George Austen to be one of the boys examined by the Skinners' appointed examiner, The Rev. Nicholas Fayting, for in a subsequent letter from George's uncle Stephen Austen to Edward Weller of Tonbridge, the London bookseller remarks,

> "… my nephew, George Austen shows away before the Skinners I understand, they praise the boy too much as indeed they did my nephew Harry (Henry Austen), it gives them a wrong turn of mind and makes them ridiculous conceited…"[26]

By 1746 the number of boys on the school roll had once again started to increase and in January 1746 Cawthorn appointed a fellow north countryman to be his assistant, or Usher. The Rev. Johnson Towers was the son of John Towers [27], a teacher, who had been teaching in Westmoreland when Cawthorn had been a pupil at Kirkby Lonsdale Grammar School in 1735. It is possible that Johnson Towers, although a few years younger than Cawthorn, was also a pupil in the same school when Cawthorn was there and the two men could therefore have known each other since childhood.

The visitation of the Skinners in May 1746 was also notable in that Cawthorn wrote a poem which was to be recited by carefully chosen boys to the visiting members of the Skinners' Company. This was the first of what became an annual tradition during Cawthorn's tenure as headmaster and the choice of topics is instructive. His selection of boys chosen to deliver the verses is also of interest, although for this first example a number of deductions need to be made in order to identify the chosen two boys, as in the compilation of Cawthorn's works published in 1771 they are identified only as "Messrs. M and A" [28]. Although there are a number of boys on the 1746 school register whose surnames begin with the letter M and who could therefore have been one of the boys speaking before the Skinners, the other boy is more easily identified. This is because at this time only two boys in the school had surnames which began with the letter A and one of these boys had only just joined and was towards the bottom of the school roll as ranked by age and ability. The other boy, who was by this time one of the most senior boys by both age and ability and was therefore the one most likely to have been chosen to speak, was George Austen. For a young orphan dependent upon the goodwill and charity of others, the choice of subject made by Cawthorn is fitting, inspired and well-timed: "The Equality of Human Conditions; A Poetical Dialogue".

The members of the Skinners' visitation delegation would undoubtedly have paused for thought when listening to some of the lines delivered by the young orphan, George Austen:

"You ask me Sir! What few were care to give,
Some grave instruction how you ought to live.
You with that envied blissful scene to find
That charms the taste, and dignifies the mind;
That nobly mingles every art to please,
And joins the majesty of life to ease.

HEAR then my friend! The doctrine I disclose,
As true as if displayed in pompous prose;
As if Locke's sacred hand the page had wrote,
And every doctor stamped it with a vote.

All lots are equal, and all states the same,
Alike in merit, tho' unlike in name.
In reasons eye no difference lies between
Life's noon-day lustres or her milder scene.
'Tis not the plate that dignifies the board,
Nor all the titles blazing round a lord.
'Tis not the splendid plume, th' embroidered vest,
The gorgeous sword-knot, or the martial crest,
That lends to life the smile, the jest, the glee:
Or makes his honour happier than me… [29]

… HEAR then, without the specious pride of art,
A truth that strikes the moral to the heart;
A truth that liv'd in Cato's patriot-breast,
And bade a dying Socrates be blest.
All, all, but virtue, is a school-boy's theme,
The air-dress'd phantom of a virgin's dream:
A gilded toy, that homebred fools desire,
That coxcombs boast of, and that mobs admire.

> Her radiant graces every bliss unfold,
> And turns whate'er she touches into gold." [30]

Thanks to some assiduous promotion by his headmaster and mentor, George Austen, the happy, talented and virtuous schoolboy "blessed with a bright and hopeful disposition" [31], was by now well known to the members of the Skinners' Company who had made the annual visitation pilgrimages to the school.

Towards the end of 1746 Cawthorn received his first rebuttal from the Skinners when an application he submitted for repairs at the school was rejected; "… it not being a proper season of the year for doing the said repairs" [32].

1747 – A Bitter/Sweet Year

In early 1747 Cawthorn again impressed and delighted the Skinners with his diligent and obedient behaviour by responding in a timely and positive manner to a request from a Committee of Leases meeting held on the 16th February that,

> "… he do before Lady Day next, cause all such windows to be stopped up as can conveniently be spared in any of the rooms belonging to the school house, his own or the Ushers apartments, or any of the buildings at the said school belonging to this Company liable to be charged by the late Act of Parliament" [33].

In carrying out this request, Cawthorn was able to mitigate the effects of the recently passed Act of Parliament which sought to raise revenue by levying an increased tax on property owners in proportion to the number of windows their properties contained – the widely despised "Window Tax". [34]

The first few years of Cawthorn's tenure as headmaster were undoubtedly a great success as he continuously impressed the Skinners, who had reluctantly, and with little choice, taken a gamble in appointing him. He also started to win back the trust and respect of parents as is evidenced by the fact that numbers on the school register had once again started to climb.

In the summer of 1747 the opportunities which Cawthorn had afforded his star pupil, George Austen, to display his talents to the visiting delegations of Skinners to the school on the annual visitation, bore fruit as Austen was rewarded with a fellowship to St John's, Oxford, reserved for a pupil from Tonbridge School [35].

Elsewhere, however, Cawthorn's memories of 1747 must have been decidedly sad for this year was marked by bitter personal tragedy. His wife, Mary, who is described as "an amiable, sensible, ingenious woman, but had long laboured under a bad state of health" [36], had given birth to a young daughter who had survived for only a few hours. The previous year she had given birth to twin daughters who had survived for little more than a couple of days and whose memory Cawthorn had commemorated in a poignant poem lamenting their short lives. This second tragedy in as many years proved too much for Mary and she also passed away, to be buried in Tonbridge Parish Church alongside her daughters. The resulting upheaval in his personal life meant that the sermon he was due to preach to the Skinners' Company on the theme of "Benevolence" was postponed to the following year. It would, of course, have been a particularly appropriate subject given the generosity shown to Austen in being awarded the White's fellowship to Oxford, but was nevertheless well enough received in 1748 for the Skinners to vote to have it published [37].

Given everything else that happened in his life, it is almost a footnote to record that Cawthorn was also awarded the degree of MA in 1747. This achievement is rather dismissively recorded by some historians, such as Chalmers, who having noted his apparent failure to complete his studies at Cambridge, comments that,

> "when promoted to the school of Tunbridge he had obtained the degree of M.A. probably from some northern university" [38].

The degree was, in fact, a Lambeth MA awarded by the Archbishop of Canterbury, Dr John Potter on the 23rd June, who,

> "… judged it expedient that you whose proficiency in the Study of Divinity, Uprigtness of Life, sound Doctrine and Purity of Morals are manifest unto us, Go dignified with the degree of Master of Arts"[39].

This was one of only two Lambeth MAs Potter awarded during 1747, the other being bestowed upon his youngest son, Thomas Potter, whose elder brother, also called John, had until 1746 been Rector of St Mary's The Virgin in Chiddingstone, near Tonbridge, where Cawthorn's father-in-law, Martin Clare, was to be subsequently buried. Earlier in his ecclesiastical career Archbishop Dr Potter had been a Chaplain-in-Waiting in the Court of Queen Anne at the same time as a distant relative of Cawthorn's, The Rev. Richard Cawthorn, had been Chaplain of the Chapel Royal at Hampton Court Palace. Potter had also written an influential book titled *A Discourse of Church Government...* [40] which had been published in 1724 by a number of prominent booksellers some of whom subsequently knew, and were known to Cawthorn. He may not have completed his studies at Cambridge University but from 1747, Cawthorn was nevertheless able to style himself MA thanks to his growing reputation... and possibly a few useful contacts.

Acceptance and Burying the Past

The first decade of James Cawthorn's headmaster's tenure passed with him keen to please his masters and both his own and the school's reputation rising steadily. He demonstrated a confident, competent character and was obedient to the wishes and directions of his employers. He was also regaining the trust of parents and the number of boys on the school register began to climb steadily, reaching fifty-seven by the summer of 1752[41]. The esteem in which the Headmaster of Tonbridge School was now held, in and around the town, was illustrated the following year through the actions of one of the area's most notable families.

The Children family had lived in the Tonbridge area for generations and Richard Children of Ramhurst Manor in the village of Leigh, near Tonbridge, had sent his sons to be educated at Tonbridge School under Cawthorn's predecessor, Richard Spencer. The eldest son, John Children, married Jane Weller, the daughter of Robert Weller of Tonbridge – a family to whom George Austen was related through his grandmother, Elizabeth Weller. They were married on the 21st February 1736 by special licence in Sir Christopher Wren's chapel at the Royal Hospital, Chelsea[42] where an Old Tonbridgian contemporary of John Children's, the Rev. William Ashburnham, occupied the post of Chaplain to the Hospital [43]. After his marriage, John Children moved to Tonbridge where he bought Ferox Hall, a manor house on the high street which was situated on the opposite side of the road from the headmaster's house and study, at Tonbridge School. John Children's only son, George, enrolled as a day boy in 1750 [44].

In 1753, Richard Children of Leigh died and his family erected a memorial to him in the parish church of Tonbridge, St Peter's and St Paul's. The marble monument to Richard Children was commissioned from the renowned French sculptor Louis Francois Roubiliac, who was a noted friend and associate of both George Frederic Handel and William Hogarth. Roubiliac was one of the most distinguished sculptors of his day and had risen to prominence in 1745 after producing a critically acclaimed funeral monument to the Duke of Argyll in Westminster Abbey. The Children family, however, in addition to commissioning the most distinguished sculptor of the period, also invited James Cawthorn to compose some verse to the memory of Richard Children which were duly incorporated by Roubiliac into his memorial work:

"O thou whose manners unadorned by Art
Ennobled e'ery virtue of the Heart
Fond to forbid in each sad Scene of Woe
The Pang to torture, and the Tear to flow,
Take from the Muse, thou lov'd this honest line,
Sacred to Goodness, and a Soul like thine.
A Soul supreme that 'midst fair Ease and Health,
The Warmth of Nature, and the Pomps of Wealth
Careless of all that wild Ambition fires
All Av'rice wishes, and all Pride admires,
Gave Year on Year beneath her genial Bay,
To melt in modest Innocence away
And made each Passion, spite of all its ways
Calm as her Sun – sat in unclouded age" [45]

Ten years after his controversial appointment as Headmaster of Tonbridge School, James Cawthorn, who since 1748 had also been curate of St Mary's Church in the village of Leigh [46], had become a highly valued and respected member of the local community of Tonbridge and its surrounding area. Any lingering concerns about the headmaster amongst either the parents of boys at Tonbridge or amongst the members of the Skinners' Company had by now been dispelled. Although he had yet to fulfil his ambitions for the school, in particular in regards to the establishment of a school library, he could look back with satisfaction on a successful first decade as headmaster.

However, a decade after his appointment, Cawthorn's personal circumstances once again changed markedly, and although the changes were in many respects as equally traumatic as some of the events of 1747, they also resulted in Cawthorn acquiring a significant degree of financial independence. This dramatic increase in his personal wealth changed his relationship with the Skinners' Company but also in turn led directly to the building of the first library at Tonbridge School. To understand the cause of these changes it is necessary to consider Cawthorn's family background in more detail.

Family Background

James Cawthorn was born on the 4th November 1719 in Sheffield [47], the son of Thomas Cawthorn, originally from Thurgoland in the West Riding of Yorkshire. The hamlet of Thurgoland lay ten miles to the north west of Sheffield on the course of the River Don, in the parish of Silkstone, a short distance from the village of Cawthorne, from where the family surname is derived. The earliest written record of the area is in the Domesday Book 1086, at which time Silkstone was part of the Saxon manor of Calthorne (Cawthorne):

> In Calthorne, Ailric had three carucates of land to be taxed and there may be two ploughs there. The same now has it of Ilbert, himself two ploughs

there, and four villanes with two ploughs. There is a priest and a church, wood pasture two miles long and two broad; the whole manor three miles long and two broad. Value in King Edwards time forty shillings, now twenty shillings. To this manor belongs Silchestone, one carucate and a half. [48].

Thomas Cawthorn married Mary Laughton [49], the daughter of a linen draper from Gainsborough, Edmund Laughton, who was the grandson of Sir Edmund Laughton. After their marriage in Gainsborough in 1716, Thomas and Mary moved to Sheffield where Thomas opened a bookshop on Angel Street [50]. Their first child, Elizabeth, was born the year after their marriage, followed by James in 1719. In all, Mary gave birth to nine children, six of whom survived into adulthood, three boys and three girls[51]. The boys were all educated at the grammar school in Sheffield, although in 1735 James was removed and sent to Kirkby Lonsdale in Westmoreland to complete his schooling [52]. On his return he worked as deputy to the headmaster in the nearby Rotherham Grammar School before he moved to Cambridge and matriculated at Clare Hall.

Although his family background appears to have been a comfortable one, it does not at first sight appear to represent the most likely source of his subsequent financial independence. This suspicion is reinforced when it is recognised that on matriculation to Cambridge, James was enrolled as a sizar – that is, a poor scholar who in return for his education, had to wait at table for the other members of college [53]. It is also the case that he did not appear to live in college but instead lodged locally. This may have been in

Cambridge or he may have stayed with some cousins who lived in the area around Cambridge. A number of Cawthorn families lived in and around Ely; and given Cawthorn's well-documented habit of riding not insignificant distances on horseback [54], it could be that financial expediency led him to stay with family as far away as Ely, whilst riding into Cambridge in order to attend college.

Cawthorn's poetry, often apparently inspired by experiences from his own life, makes a playful reference to his old college when, the same learned and academic character who "often dropped in at Hitch's shop", had earlier in the same poem,

"... the luck to fall
Plump in the area of Clare Hall
Just as old Wilcox, from a slope
Was gazing thro' his telescope" [55]

His poetry is, however, singularly unhelpful when trying to identify the source of his independent wealth, although it does, nevertheless, hint at some intriguing possibilities; for despite being ordained into the priesthood and gambling being specifically outlawed in the Tonbridge School statutes, where it is clearly stated "... that the Master and Usher shall neither of them be a common gamester... "[56], Cawthorn appears to have enjoyed the occasional flutter:

"Cawthorn had once a mind to fix
His carcass in a coach and six
And live, if his estate would bear it,

> On turtle, ortolans, and claret,
> For this he went, at fortune's call,
> To wait upon her at Guildhall;
> That is, like many other thick wits,
> He bought a score of Lottery Tickets" [57]

Unfortunately, this does not appear to be the answer to the question about the source of Cawthorn's independent wealth, for the poem continues,

> "And saw them rise in dreadful ranks
> Converted to a score of blanks" [58]

In fact, in order to uncover the mystery of where Cawthorn acquired his wealth, it is necessary to look in more detail at his father, Thomas, and his various business interests in and around the city of Sheffield in the early eighteenth century.

From Bookshops to Lead Mines

James Cawthorn's father, Thomas, would most likely be described as a "serial entrepreneur" if he were alive today. He is instead usually referred to as either an "upholsterer" or a "cabinet-maker". The bookshop he operated on Angel Street in Sheffield is also sometimes mentioned in accounts of his life:

> "…Thomas Cawthorne, born in 1687, established himself on the west side of Angel Street, just above the 'Angel Inn', apparently combining

with an upholsterer's business some dabbling in bookselling" [59].

In fact, the most appropriate description to use when describing Thomas' principle form of employment would probably be the old-fashioned term used for an artisan employed as an upholsterer or cabinet-maker, that is – an upholder. The most detailed contemporary description of the role of an upholder is found in Robert Campbell's *The London Tradesman* published in 1747:

> I have just finished my House and must now think of furnishing it with fashionable furniture. The Upholder is Chief Agent in this case. He is the Man upon whose judgement I rely in the Choice of Goods; and I suppose he has not only judgement in the Materials, but taste in the Fashions, and Skill in the Workmanship. This Tradesman's Genius must be universal in every Branch of Furniture… He was originally a Species of the Taylor; but by degrees, has crept over his Head, and set up as a Connoisseur in every article that belongs to the House. He employs Journeymen in his own proper Calling, Cabinet-Makers, Glass-Grinders, Looking-Glass Frame Carvers, Carvers for Chairs, Testers and Posts for Beds, the Woollen-Draper, the Mercer, the Linen-Draper, several Species of Smiths, and a vast many tradesmen of the other mechanic Branches. The Upholder, according to this Description of his Business must be no fool; and have a considerable Stock to set up with."[60]

Campbell goes on to suggest that the amount of capital required to set up as an upholder could be anything up to £1000[61]. This figure could be doubled if the artisan concerned was also engaged in cabinet-making in his own right [62]. These are not inconsiderable sums for the eighteenth century when, for example, by way of comparison, the annual cost of educating a boy at Tonbridge School was of the order of £20-£30 a year [63].

It is possible that Thomas Cawthorn received some financial assistance to initially enable him to set up shop as an upholder, perhaps from his wife's family. There is much evidence, however, to suggest that, once established, Thomas Cawthorn was a very successful upholder – not least in the fact that he could afford to send his sons to the grammar school in Sheffield for their education. His work as a tradesman was not, however, his only involvement in the business environment that characterised Sheffield at this time.

Sheffield was a city that was growing rapidly and moving away from a traditional focus as a regional market town into a position as a nationally important centre for a range of manufactured goods built around the strength of its position in the cutlery trade. The development of Sheffield in the eighteenth century was accompanied by a wave of entrepreneurial spirit which saw many of the city's citizens engaged in a range of more or less speculative business ventures. Thomas Cawthorn played a full part in some of these endeavours and took a particularly active interest in a number of mining projects – specifically lead mining. This is hardly surprising given lead's role and use as something of a "wonder" material in the eighteenth century building trade and recognising Thomas' tangential interest in this sector.

From Lead Mines to Legacies

Unfortunately, Thomas' first foray into lead mining in the 1720s resulted in feuding over the rights to develop a seam of ore to the south of Sheffield in an area known as Wardlow Moor. He and his fellow "adventurers" from Sheffield agreed terms with the local freeholder the Duke of Devonshire and with his tenants to allow them to exploit the lead deposits on their land. However, a rival group of local adventurers claimed that the lead was actually on land over which they, in fact, held the mineral rights, and after these interlopers had occupied the mine, Thomas and his partners,

> "… found that great quantities of lead ore had been got in and taken out of the same works and sold and carried away" [64].

When they challenged this activity, the Sheffield adventurers were told in no uncertain terms by the local interlopers that if they,

> "… or any person on their behalf came there they would hold them back and oppose them by force"[65].

With what was very quickly turning into an ugly situation, the protagonists agreed to litigation in order to resolve the stand-off and a local court was convened in order to arbitrate. The customs and proceedings, however, appear to have been stacked in favour of the local men and the Sheffield adventurers eventually lost all their rights to the mine.

One of Thomas' partners, George Steer, was so incensed by the treatment of the mining "adventurers" from Sheffield in what he considered to be a number of "sham trials" that he resolved to produce a definitive and unambiguous account of the laws and customs covering mining activities in the "High Peak" district. His stated aim in the preface to his resulting compendium was,

"… to keep peace, and preserve the Miners Property, that their Rights may not be taken from them; to be a Direction to Juries on Trials; and to Grand Juries… that Justice may be done… at all Mine-Trials" [66].

His book *The Compleat Mineral Laws…* was published in 1734 by the eminent London publisher Henry Woodfall, the friend and associate of Martin Clare's patron, Sir Arthur Onslow. The book was distributed by booksellers serving both the London legal profession and the mining communities of Derbyshire and Yorkshire.

Thomas Cawthorn, meanwhile, was not a man who could be easily deterred. In the autumn of 1730 a local landowner Nicholas Stead approached him with the claim that "he had reason to believe there was a great quantity of lead ore" [67] on his land. The land in question was in an area called Bytham's in the district of Bradfield, to the north-west of Sheffield. Records dating back to the English Civil War [68] identify this area as a lead producing region and Thomas therefore had no reason to doubt the authenticity of the claim. During 1731 he and a number of other Sheffield 'adventurers' set up a 'co-partnership' to develop a mine in which Thomas was the dominant partner with a shareholding amounting to over forty per cent of the venture [69]. Lead mining was soon underway and it very quickly became clear that the ore body also extended under the land of adjacent landowners. Side agreements were established with these owners in which they were effectively paid a lease to allow the mine to extend under their property [70].

With what was clearly developing into a quite substantial mining operation it was not long before disputes arose and in 1735 litigation once again ensued[71]. This time, however, and probably in part due to the important legal precedents which had been established after the publication by Henry Woodfall of George Steer's *Compleat Mineral Laws...* the proceedings went in favour of Thomas' consortium of adventurers and their rights were upheld. The mine continued to flourish throughout the rest of his life with shares in the venture occasionally changing hands "for a full and valuable consideration" [72].

Thomas Cawthorn's lead mines formed the basis of his and his family's prosperity for the rest of his life and would indirectly continue to support his family long after his death.

1754 – A Year of Change

James Cawthorn's father, Thomas, died in 1754. In his will his instructions to his executors were "that his goods and chattels remain as they are… as long as my wife shall live" [73]. On his wife's death his goods were to be sold and the proceeds distributed equally amongst his surviving children. This was, however, with the exception of his interest in the mine at Bytham's which was to be sold immediately "with all its rights and privileges… to the best bidder"[74]. Thomas "desires that"[75] his son James will assist the executors in this task.

Historical evidence of how much the interest in the lead mine sold for is sadly lacking. Nevertheless, accounts of the financially comfortable lives subsequently lived by Thomas' children, and indeed his grandchildren, suggest that they must have each inherited a significant capital sum. The wealth inherited from the proceeds of the sale of the lead mines was not always immediately obvious however, as, for example, in the case of Edward Goodwin, only child of James Cawthorn's sister Elizabeth, who "although a bachelor, and reputed wealthy" [76] was not known for his generosity. That is though,

> … until the day of his funeral, when large numbers of poor recipients of his secret bounty attended to mourn their benefactor and testify their gratitude, was it discovered how cruelly the world had wronged him, for he had done good by stealth, and had quietly given away to the indigent the whole of his property, except £2000 which he left to an orphan girl whom he had maintained after the death of her father. [77]

It is clear that 1754 was a pivotal year in James Cawthorn's life. His father's death resulted in James receiving a financial windfall in the form of an inheritance that secured his financial independence.

Building Foundations

The sale of his father's lead mines was the source of James Cawthorn's independent wealth. The inheritance he received on his father's death created the foundations upon which James' life would now develop. The independence that his new-found wealth brought him was instrumental in enabling Cawthorn to finally begin work on laying the foundations for the first library building at Tonbridge School.

CHAPTER FOUR

Building the Library

The inheritance that James Cawthorn received on the sale of the lead mines in Yorkshire, after the death of his father in 1754, transformed his life. He became financially independent and would use his new-found wealth to good effect. His independence would, however, have a profound effect on his relationship with the Skinners' Company.

1754 – A Year of Change

James Cawthorn had remained close to his family back in Yorkshire and felt the loss of his father deeply. Meanwhile, the death of his brother Thomas [1] in the same year deprived James of a sibling who was also a close friend and confidant and with whom he probably stayed during his visits to London. Shortly after Thomas Junior's death, his younger brother Charles took over the business in Leadenhall Market, and Land Registry records identify Charles taking over Thomas' premises during the course of the year [2]. As was the case with Thomas, Charles was also admitted to the Freedom of the Skinners' Company as is evident in the following entry for a Court of Assistants meeting held on the 17th May 1754:

> "Ordered that Mr Charles Cawthorne of Leadenhall Street, Hardwareman be admitted into the Freedom of this Company by Redemption upon his paying the usual and accustomed fees" [3].

Over the course of the next twenty years Charles would play an increasing role in the affairs of the Worshipful Company of Skinners, being elected Renter Warden in June 1772 [4].

There were other changes in James Cawthorn's life too in 1754, when his Usher for the previous seven years, Johnson Towers, resigned from his post. The circumstances appear to have been unfortunate. Cawthorn's deputy was called upon to give the Election Day sermon before the Skinners, and afterwards he asked for payment of ten guineas to cover his expenses. This is what had always been paid as evidenced by the records in the Skinners' Payments Ledgers and there is therefore nothing unusual in the claim. However, the Skinners' Court records hint at a dispute over the payment to Towers when the following entries for the 24th October 1754 are recorded:

> "Ordered that ten guineas be taken out of this Company's cash and given to Mr Johnson Towers towards defraying his expenses in giving his sermon preached before this Company on their election day, being the 13th day of June last, but this to be no precedent" [5].

Furthermore, it is added that,

> "A motion being made that if any member of this Court for the future shall direct any expense to be made without an order of this Court for that purpose, that this Company shall not be charged therewith" [6].

It was also made clear that this would not be the end of the matter for it is,

> "Ordered that the further consideration these of be referred to the next Court" [7].

Perhaps there was a misunderstanding, or maybe the sermon was just not very good. Either way, Towers resigned shortly afterwards. This additional upheaval in Cawthorn's life was clearly unwelcome and unhelpful, but it was perhaps inevitable that in his hour of need, help was at hand in the person of George Austen who returned from Oxford in order to replace Towers as Cawthorn's deputy.

The trauma in James Cawthorn's personal life during 1754 clearly had an impact on his work at Tonbridge for this is one of the few years during his tenure as headmaster when a list of the pupils present at the school was not produced.

So it was that as the undoubtedly traumatic year of 1754 drew to a close, James Cawthorn's personal and professional life had both undergone fundamental change. In his family life he had lost both his father and one of his younger brothers, and at Tonbridge he had accepted the resignation of the first and only Usher he had appointed to date. However, as a result of his father's death and the sale of the lead mines, which resulted in significant inheritances for

Thomas Cawthorn's surviving children, James Cawthorn would begin 1755 with an unfamiliar level of financial independence. He also had a new deputy in George Austen who was not only familiar with the school and how it operated, but was also a product of Cawthorn's own teaching methods. Cawthorn's losses were to be Tonbridge's gain and the school's library would be the immediate beneficiary.

Work finally begins on the first library building at Tonbridge School

During 1755 the routine of life at Tonbridge School re-established an equilibrium, and by the beginning of 1756 Cawthorn made it clear what he intended doing with his new-found financial freedom when he submitted a proposal to the Skinners' Company to pull down the old headmaster's study and rebuild it. Although not mentioned explicitly, the new, larger study was to be used to house the school's rapidly expanding collection of books. Tonbridge School would finally get its first library building.

At a Court of Assistants meeting held on the 28th January 1756,

> "A letter from the Rev. Mr Cawthorne, Master of Tunbridge School together with an estimate thereto annexed of the charge of pulling down and New Building the Masters Study at the school in manner therein described amounting to the sum of fifty nine pounds, fifteen shillings and eleven pence, was read" [8].

The new study-cum-library was to be built "in the Grecian style" [9] and after some debate the Skinners approved the plans. However, no doubt mindful of the manner in which major building works had a tendency to overshoot their initial funding estimates, they imposed a limit on how much the Skinners' Company would be prepared to pay and any overspend was to be met from the headmaster's own resources. Such caution is hardly surprising given the perennial lack of funds from which the Skinners suffered and Cawthorn's previously demonstrated inclination to do what he thought was right for the school regardless of the ultimate cost, which he would present to the Skinners in the expectation that they would always find the necessary funds. Emboldened by his new-found affluence, Cawthorn was happy to agree to the conditions imposed, and so it was,

> "Ordered that the said study be pulled down and new built according to the said estimate and that a sum of money not exceeding sixty pounds be paid to the said Mr Cawthorne to defray the expenses thereof, upon his producing sufficient vouchers to the Company that the same have been laid out accordingly" [10].

Hence, in the spring of 1756, work finally started on the construction of what would become the first library building at Tonbridge School.

The work would take most of the year to complete, but in the meantime school life continued as normal during the construction phase. The annual visitation conducted on the 27th May resulted in a subsequent Committee of Leases meeting held on the 9th July approving funds to cover additional "work done at the school house" [11] amounting to the sum of a little over twenty one pounds; and the usual annual gratuities given to Cawthorn and his deputy, George Austen, were also approved and paid after the visitation.

Cawthorn also used the occasion of the visitation of 1756 to good effect in ensuring that the library, then under construction, would be built to his specifications. Once again he used his poetry, written for the visitation, and this time recited by Samuel Gordon [12], to convey a message to the visiting Skinners. The first clue as to content is in the title to that year's poem, *On Taste – An Essay*, and the verse makes clear the headmaster's firmly held views on what constituted appropriate style and taste in matters of architecture and design. Cawthorn, for example, praised the popular use of classical Roman and Greek style in ensuring that natural light flooded the interior of church buildings – a natural light, which was diffused by the design of the windows of the church. He was not necessarily, however, a passionate proponent of such architectural style when actually used for church buildings:

'One might expect a sanity of style,
August and manly in an holy pile,
And think an architect extremely odd
To build a playhouse for the church of God:
Yet half our church's, such the mode that reigns,
Are Roman theatres, or Grecian fanes;
Where broad arch'd windows to the eye convey
The keen diffusion of too strong a day;

> Where, in the luxury of wanton pride,
> Corinthian columns languish side by side…" [13]

He also dismissed as a passing fad, the then popularity in matters of architecture, design and landscaping of all things Chinese,

> "… Of late, tis true, quite sick of Rome, and Greece,
> We fetch our models from the wise Chinese:
> European artists are too cool, and chaste,
> For Mand'rin only is the man of taste;
> Whose bolder genius, fondly wild to see
> His grove a forest, and his pond a sea,
> Breaks out – and, whimsically great, designs
> Without the shackles or of rules, or lines:
> Form'd on his plans, our farms and seats begin
> To match the boasted villas of Pekin (Beijing)" [14]

… before he makes it clear that whilst there is a time and a place for a range of competing architectural styles and fashions, the Tonbridge School library would be built in a refined, elegant and tasteful form – one determined by the headmaster:

> "… Peace to all such – but you whose (virtue) fires
> True greatness kindles, and true sense inspires,
> Or ere you lay a stone, or plant a shade,
> Bend the proud arch, or roll the broad cascade,
> Ere all your wealth in mean profusion waste,
> Examine nature with the eye of Taste…

> ... (For) Taste corrects, by one eternal touch,
> What seems too little, and what seems too much,
> Marks the fine point where each consenting part
> Slides into beauty with the ease of art;
> This, bids to rise, and that with grace to fall,
> And bounds, unites, refines, and heightens all." [15]

This was Cawthorn at his best: confident, uncompromising and assertive. Tonbridge School would get its first library building during his tenure as headmaster, and it would be one designed and built by the son of an upholder: a man who was confident that he knew what he was talking about when it came to architecture and understood what constituted an appropriate style for a new library. This would be a building his father, whose lead mines in Yorkshire were underwriting the library's construction, would have been proud to witness. Tall, elegant, imposing columns – a building finished in a classical Grecian style, boasting an interior flooded with natural light, ingeniously diffused in such a way as to protect the books within.

The new Tonbridge School library was the Rev. James Cawthorn's library in every sense: his Temple for the Worship of Books.

However, in the summer of 1756, whilst Cawthorn's library was under construction, storm clouds were gathering. Events occurred which, although totally unrelated to the building works then underway in Tonbridge, would when taken together with the circumstances under which the first school library was built, have important implications for Tonbridge School, its headmaster and his still relatively new deputy, George Austen.

Developments at the Foundling Hospital

In the summer of 1756 the charitable institution in London known as the Foundling Hospital was in serious financial difficulty. It had been established in 1741 by the philanthropic retired sea captain Thomas Coram, who had been appalled by the number of illegitimate children he had witnessed abandoned each year on the streets of the capital. Initially located in Hatton Garden, Coram's home for these abandoned infants, or foundlings as they were known, attracted the backing of a number of important benefactors, most notably William Hogarth and George Frederic Handel and later including the likes of Sir Joshua Reynolds and Thomas Gainsborough. Using the benefits of such high profile endorsements, funds were raised in 1742 to construct a purpose-built refuge. The Foundling Hospital, as the new home was called, was situated on land in Bloomsbury, to the north of Great Ormond Street. The first wing opened in 1745 and a separate wing for girls opened in 1752. However, relying as it did on charitable donations, the finances of the hospital were never on a secure footing, despite the best efforts of its principle supporters and the Governors were eventually forced to seek government support.

The childless Handel in particular, who had paid the school fees of his secretary's son in order for John Christopher Smith to attend the Soho Academy, had been a tireless supporter of the home for abandoned children. In 1750 he had directed a performance of his *Messiah* to mark the occasion of the installation of an organ in the hospital chapel and such was the success of the concert he had repeated it in subsequent years. On the 7th April 1756 a meeting of the Committee for "Transacting the Affairs of the Foundling Hospital"[16] was informed that Handel had agreed to direct another performance of *Messiah* for the benefit of the hospital. The performance was to take place on the 19th May and 1200 tickets were to be sold through a number of coffee houses with advertisements for such tickets placed in the *Daily Advertiser, Public Advertiser, London Evening Post* and the *Whitehall Evening Post*. Such advertisements were duly placed with the following appearing in the *Daily Advertiser*:

> "Hospital for the Maintenance and Education of exposed and deserted young Children;This is to give Notice that, under the direction of GEORGE FREDERICK HANDEL, Esq; the Sacred Oratorio, called MESSIAH, will be perform'd in the Chapel of this Hospital, for the Benefit of this Charity, Tomorrow, the 19th of this instant, at Twelve o'Clock at Noon, precisely. To prevent the Chapel being crowded, the Gentlemen are desired to come without Swords, and the Ladies without Hoops." [17]

In the event, nearly 1400 tickets were sold and given that James Cawthorn, "had been known to ride from Tonbridge to London, to hear a concert, between the afternoon of one day and seven o'clock in the morning of the next" [18], it is quite possible that the Headmaster of Tonbridge School, perhaps accompanied by his deputy, George Austen, was in the audience. It is certainly the case that Cawthorn was familiar with the works of Handel for he later used references to the composer's genius in order to illustrate a point about the pursuit of happiness delivered in one of his poems on a subsequent Skinners' Day visitation:

> "Irregularly will (mankind's) passions roll
> Thro' nature's finest instrument, the soul:
> While men of sense, with Handel's happier skill,
> Correct the taste, and harmonize the will,
> Teach their affections like his notes to flow,
> Not rais'd too high, nor ever sunk too low;
> Till every virtue, measur'd and refin'd,
> As fits the concert of the master-mind,
> Melts in its kindred sounds, and pours along,
> Th' according music of the moral song" [19]

The popular and well-attended concert raised over £660, after costs, for the hospital [20]. More importantly however, on the 21st May, two days after the performance, the House of Commons voted to provide £10,000 of public money to the Foundling Hospital in order to enable the institution to receive all abandoned children under the age of two months old. The number of children presented to the hospital would soon experience exponential growth.

Events now moved very quickly and at a meeting held on the 24th May the Governors decided that part of the new funds should be used to build an infirmary and nursery for the hospital[21]. Many of the children presented to the hospital were quite sickly and it was important to reduce the risk of epidemics taking hold in the institution; the proposed infirmary was to play a key role in this regard. Unfortunately however, the hospital was quickly outgrowing its existing site and so it was decided to approach the owners of adjoining land with an offer or proposal, known as a "Memorial", to purchase their land and in thus doing, so enable the Foundling to expand. The most suitably located adjoining land was an area known as the Sandhills Estate owned by The Worshipful Company of Skinners.

The Sandhills Estate

The Sandhills Estate was an area of land predominantly used for pasture in 1756 and was located to the north of the Foundling Hospital, extending into the parish of St Pancras. It had been purchased by Sir Andrew Judd and was leased to a number of smallholders. On Sir Andrew's death, his will had provided for the land to be placed in trust and the rents from the leaseholds were to be used for the purpose of supporting the costs of running Tonbridge School. This arrangement had been enshrined in two Acts of Parliament enacted during the reign of Queen Elizabeth I.

The Governors of the Foundling Hospital, at a meeting held on Wednesday 14th July 1756 agreed that,

"… a Memorial be presented to the Master and Wardens and Court of Assistants of the Skinner's Company"… seeking to purchase… "the Estate belonging to Your Worshipful Company, called Sandhills, adjoining to the Estate of your Memorialist… at such price as this Company shall said to be a reasonable Equivalent for the same" [22].

The approach from the Governors of the Foundling Hospital is recorded in the Skinners' Court records with an entry for a Court of Assistants meeting held the following day on the 15th July, when the following was noted:

"… request from the Foundling Hospital to purchase Sandhills Estate to build an Infirmary and Nurseries for the Foundling Hospital" [23].

The fortuitous timing of the approach was not lost on the members of the Court of Assistants; on the one hand, the Skinners' Company's neighbours, the Foundling Hospital, had received a significant injection of capital, some of which they wished to use in order to purchase the Sandhills Estate for a "full and valuable" consideration. On the other hand, The Skinners were, as usual, short of money to support their school in Tonbridge at a time when the number of boys at the school was once again increasing and the headmaster was so eager to expand and develop the school he had undertaken to underwrite, with his own money, a new library building currently being constructed. The Sandhills Estate had been left in trust to the Skinners specifically in order to support Tonbridge School. The potential to conclude a mutually beneficial transaction was obvious and, as such, the request was delegated to the Committee of Leases, with instructions to investigate the potential for a sale,

"… free from any breach of the Trusts in the Will of Sir Andrew Judd" [24].

The members of the Committee of Leases, on the 21st July 1756 "… departed to take a view of the said premises" [25] before reconvening on the 28th July where it was,

> "Resolved that it is the opinion of this Committee that for the reasons in the said memorial set forth, this Company do contract and agree with the said Hospital for the sale of the said Estate for a valuable consideration" [26].

However, it is also clear from the court records that there were some serious misgivings as to whether or not the Skinners' Company actually had a mandate that would allow them to conclude a satisfactory sale to the Foundling Hospital because at the same meeting it was also,

> "Ordered that Office copys be procured of the two Acts of Parliament of the 14th and 31st of Queen Elizabeth, the One, intitled 'An Act for Assuring Lands for the Free Grammar School of Tunbridge in Kent' and the other intitled 'An Act for the Better Assurance of Lands and Tenements to the Maintenance of the Grammar School of Tunbridge in the County of Kent'" [27].

There was quite clearly concern amongst at least some of the Skinners as to whether or not the Skinners' Company could actually sell the land which had been placed in trust for the benefit of Tonbridge School and over which the Skinners were merely trustees or guardians as opposed to actual owners. There was also the question of what should legally happen to the funds arising from any sale of the Sandhills Estate – would the Skinners have authority over it or would it pass to the school, in which case it would come under the control of the headmaster.

Completing the Library Building

The debate about what to do with the Sandhills Estate occupied the members of the Skinners' Company throughout the late summer of 1756, during which time the building work on the new library continued uninterrupted. It was not until a Court of Assistants meeting held on the 27th October that the issues were finally brought to a head and decisions made. It is also clear from the minutes of the meeting that the debate surrounding Sandhills continued even during the meeting and, unusually for these gatherings, this issue was finally resolved only by putting the matter to a formal vote when,

> "It being moved and the question being put whether this Company should dispose of their Estate called Sandhills to the Foundling Hospital"[28].

The motion was put to the vote and the wishes of the majority of members present at the meeting upheld when, as is stated in the minutes,

> "It passed in the negative" [29].

It was clear that the new and recently completed library would not be paid for from the proceeds of the sale of the Sandhills Estate.

This decision was immediately passed to the Foundling representatives present at Skinners' Hall that day, for at a committee meeting held at the hospital on the same day, the following entry appears in the minutes book:

> "Mr White reported from the Committee appointed to treat with the Court of Assistants of the Skinner's Company for their land adjoining to the land of the Hospital… they had resolved at present not to dispose of the said land" [30].

However, the obvious disagreement within the Skinners' Company about the decision is also noted, for it is added that,

> "… there appeared to be some Diversity of Opinion in the said Company" [31].

The differences in opinion noted by the Foundling representatives do not, however, appear to be the result of any disappointment with the price being offered for the land and it is clear that given the building commitments of Tonbridge School at this time, a timely injection of capital would have been very helpful. The issue instead appears to be a disagreement in principle within the Skinners' Company as to whether or not they actually had the authority to conclude such a sale. This becomes clear from a further consideration of the Foundling Hospital minutes from which it is also clear that the hospital were not going to take this rejection as a final answer, for at the same meeting at which the news of the Skinners' decision is announced it is,

> "Resolved that a further application be made to the said Company... " in order to encourage... "them to reconsider the said resolution" [32].

Furthermore, the Foundling Hospital members also resolve to try to canvass individual members of the Skinners' Company and to this end instruct,

> "... that the Secretary to procure a List of the Master Wardens and the Court of Assistants" [33].

The Foundling Hospital records demonstrate not only a determination by the hospital to persevere with their efforts to buy the Sandhills Estate but also indicate that they have a comprehensive knowledge of the financial pressures the Skinners are under at this time.

The work on the new library at Tonbridge School was completed in the autumn of 1756. The completion of the construction work on the library and the Foundling Hospital's understanding of the internal financial pressures within the Skinners' Company are not unrelated.

Paying for the new library

The reason the Foundling Hospital trustees appeared to have such a clear understanding of the internal finances of the Skinners' Company can be found by a further consideration of the minutes of the Court of Assistants meeting held at Skinners' Hall on the 27th October 1756, reported on by Mr White of the Foundling Hospital. This was the meeting at which the Foundling Hospital's approach was rejected when the vote "passed in the negative", and they were informed accordingly of the committee's deliberations. For it is at this very same, and somewhat discordant, committee meeting that the subject of the funding of the new Tonbridge School library was also considered. The reason this was the case was a submission by Cawthorn of the final figures for the expenditure he had incurred in completing the building works. Whether by accident or design, Cawthorn had completed the building work on the new library building just as the Skinners were due to vote on the potential sale of property which had been entrusted to the Company, for the benefit of Tonbridge School.

It is apparent from the records that the building costs may indeed have exceeded the agreed budget, in which case Cawthorn would have been obliged to make up the difference:

> "The Voucher sent by the Rev. Mr Cawthorne, Master of the School at Tunbridge to show that the sum of sixty pound hath been laid out in pulling down and rebuilding the study at the said school. Ordered that the sum of sixty pounds be paid to the said Mr Cawthorne to defray the expenses thereof pursuant to an order of Court made the 28th Day of January last" [34].

The phrase "defray the expenses" can be interpreted in a number of ways, of course. It may merely mean that the Skinners were approving the repayment of costs incurred by Cawthorn who, having taken note of the wording of the original "order of court", had spent up to the maximum allowance of sixty pounds. On the other hand, it may well mean that the building works had indeed overrun their initial cost estimates and the headmaster had, as a consequence, been obliged to cover the balance out of his own pocket.

It is hardly surprising therefore that there was a "diversity of opinion" amongst the Skinners; for they had at the same meeting, rejected an opportunity to raise a significant amount of capital for their school in Tonbridge, whilst also voting through a resolution which, in effect, enforced an obligation on the headmaster to underwrite the development of the school's estate from his own resources.

This did not mark the end of this matter.

Repercussions

The Foundling Hospital continued to press the Skinners over their desire to purchase the latter's interest in the Sandhills Estate. They were clearly aware that the principle impediment to a sale was the Skinners' concern over their legal obligations in respect of the terms of Sir Andrew Judd's bequest. This is evident from the minutes of a Foundling Governors' meeting held on the 26th January 1757[35] when the discussion appears to have revolved around trying to investigate the possibility of asking Parliament to intervene by, in effect, annulling the terms of the two Acts of Parliament passed during Queen Elizabeth's reign, governing the management of the properties bequeathed to Tonbridge School. This, it was hoped, could be done by inserting a clause in the Act of Parliament which had approved the granting of the £10,000 of public money to the hospital which, in effect, would legally require that part of the funds would have to be paid to the Skinners who would in return be legally obliged to transfer the Sandhills Estate to the Foundling Hospital, hence nullifying the previous acts. The discussion surrounding this attempted "compulsory purchase" proposal was summarised in the minutes to the meeting when it was,

"Resolved that it be an instruction to this committee applying to Parliament to consider of the means to get inserted in the Act of Parliament for enlarging the Power granted by the late Act in favour of the Hospital to enable this Corporation to purchase from the Skinner's Company to alienate the Estate called Sandhills to this Corporation" [36].

In the meantime, they also attempted to buy out some of the Skinners' tenants on the estate when, for example, the minutes of a committee meeting held on the 13th December 1756 record that it was resolved,

"… that it be recommended to the General Court to empower this committee to treat for and purchase the Estate of the Skinner's Company called the Sandhills and devised by them to Mr Roberts, which lease his now belonging to his widow and two sons" [37].

The effect of the persistent attention of the Foundling Hospital on the affairs of the Skinners' Company combined with the entrepreneurial and increasingly proprietorial approach of Tonbridge School's headmaster in building the school's first library meant that the year 1756 was an uncomfortable year for the Skinners' Company. As the year drew to a close, Tonbridge School finally had a "room for books", but only because of the forcefulness of its headmaster who underwrote the financial risk himself and part funded the building works. The Skinners had also tried and failed to sell the Sandhills Estate to the Foundling Hospital. These two events when taken together had combined to highlight the less than robust state of the Skinners' financial position and at a Court of Assistants meeting held on the 10th December it is clear from the minutes that the members had decided it was time to do something about this increasingly unsatisfactory state of affairs.

In the first instance the Committee of Leases were instructed to review the Company's property holdings and tenancy agreements and in particular to examine,

"… into the arrears which were outstanding at Midsummer last" [38].

Attention then turned from the revenue account to the expenses ledger and it was:

"Ordered that it be referred to a committee of leases to examine into the Exhibitions in the Gift of this Company and if they shall be of the opinion that any of them ought to be declared vacant that they do report the same to the Court together with the reasons for such their opinion and where they shall find any considerable arrears standing in the name of any Exhibitioner that they do enquire into the reasons thereof and if they shall be of opinion that the person in whose name such arrears stand is not properly intitled to receive it that they do report the same to the Court together with the reasons for such their opinion."[39]

This new-found determination on the part of the Skinners' Company to put their financial affairs in order coincided with a more proprietorial approach to Tonbridge School and a less deferential attitude towards the Skinners from the financially independent Cawthorn. This potentially incendiary combination would prove to be an inflammatory cocktail for the headmaster and his deputy, George Austen.

The first library building at Tonbridge School

As the year 1756 drew to a close, Tonbridge School finally had its first recognisable school library building. Although it was built as a new study for the headmaster who had overseen and underwritten its construction, it would nevertheless be referred to for the next one hundred years as the Cawthorn Library.

Its conception and construction had not, however, been without some controversy. The Skinners' Company had been divided by the debate surrounding the future of the Sandhills Estate and the less than robust state of the Company's finances had also been exposed. The year 1757 would witness a root and branch review of the Skinners' financial accounts and the saga surrounding the building of the first library at the Company's school in Tonbridge was the catalyst for this investigation.

Beyond the Building Saga

The building of the first library at Tonbridge School in 1756 had resulted in the exposure of the weak state of the Skinners' Company finances which in turn led to a wholesale review of the financial affairs of the Company. This review began almost immediately after the Court of Assistants meeting at which the approach to buy the Sandhills Estate by the Foundling Hospital was rejected, and at which James Cawthorn had been obliged to cover the overspend on the building of the school library. However, as 1757 progressed, the momentum behind the financial investigation was given added impetus when at a Court of Assistants meeting held on the 9th June, 1757 it was,

"… announced that Sir Charles Asgill, Knight and Alderman, a member of this Company is next turn to be Elected Lord Mayor – it being a good many years since there hath been any Lord Mayor of this Company" [40].

It was a great honour for a Livery Company when one of its own was elected as Lord Mayor of London, but it usually also signified a year of much increased expense. Livery Companies had traditionally competed with one another in ostentatious and expensive displays of their wealth during the twelve months that they held office. The saga surrounding the building of the first library at Tonbridge School may well have been the catalyst which prompted the Skinners to get their financial affairs into order, but the election of Sir Charles Asgill as Lord Mayor of London would give an added urgency to the investigation. The Worshipful Company of Skinners did not wish to be found wanting during Sir Charles's year in office and despite Charles Asgill being an Old Tonbridgian [41], the Skinners' Company's financial inquisition would have important implications for Tonbridge School.

First, however, it is necessary to consider further the development of the school library, and in particular, to look more closely at its other major element: the books; for of course, a "room for books", without books, is nothing more than an empty space.

CHAPTER FIVE
Developing Literary Connections

Building the first school library at Tonbridge was undoubtedly a major achievement. Cawthorn had succeeded where his predecessors had failed and in 1756 Tonbridge School finally had its first recognisable school library building. This does not of itself, however, offer a satisfactory explanation of James Cawthorn's subsequent reputation as a disciplinary despot. Indeed, given that the financial risk of building the library was underwritten by the headmaster and that it also appears, at least in part, to have been funded from the headmaster's own resources, it would seem reasonable to expect that posterity would hold him in high esteem rather than demonise his character in the way that has occurred. To understand why Cawthorn has been treated in the manner that he has by successive historians of the school it is necessary to look at the other major component of the school library – the books; after all, a library without books is merely an empty space. More specifically, it is necessary to consider the question of how Cawthorn went about the task of adding to the modest collection of books he inherited at the time he was appointed as headmaster. Although the price of books was falling, they were still expensive items to purchase. Procuring enough books to firmly establish a school library, and on a scale sufficient to necessitate the construction of a new building capable of housing such an extended collection, must have cost a lot of money. More money than was ever likely to have been raised from Spencer's Library Subscription Roll or the sixpence each boy paid into the School Box on joining the school. It is the way in which Cawthorn went about the task of procuring books for the Tonbridge School library and the precedent that he set which is the root cause of his subsequent reputation as an almost despotic disciplinarian.

From Poetry to Publishers

Prior to becoming Headmaster of Tonbridge, James Cawthorn was more widely known as an aspiring poet. According to his elder sister Elizabeth, a young James displayed early literary talent whilst at Sheffield Grammar School with an attempt to begin a periodical called *The Tea Table* [1]. The name appears to have been "borrowed from Mrs Haywood" [2] and it seems, both in style and content, to have been based on the like-named periodical in London written by Eliza Haywood. However, whilst satirical depictions of prominent thinly disguised public figures brought Haywood a certain popular notoriety in London, Cawthorn's attempts at caricaturing local worthies in Sheffield merely upset the neighbours. His business-minded father who "… thought he was too young for an observer of men and manners, and too ignorant of the world to become its advisor" [3] soon ensured that this early foray into public writing was short-lived.

Cawthorn's introduction to the works of Eliza Haywood may well have come through his father's Wardlow Moor business partner George Steer and his relationship with the London publisher Henry Woodfall. Woodfall published a number of works by Haywood including, for example, *Memories of a Certain Island adjacent to the Kingdom of Utopia*, published in 1726 [4]. Haywood's *Tea Table* periodical, however, was published by James Roberts, a Master Publisher and the outstanding trade publisher of the early eighteenth century [5]. Roberts also printed first editions for the likes of Pope, Fielding, Steele, Defoe, Prior, Swift, Young, Congreve, Addison and Dr Samuel Johnson. He had an extensive nationwide network of bookseller distributors. This eclectic but, for the most part, highbrow selection of writers may well have appealed to the part-time bookseller, Thomas Cawthorn of Angel Street. It does seem that from the earliest days of bookselling in Sheffield the proprietors of the bookshops made little effort to cater for a somewhat limited local market and instead bought books which appealed to themselves and their families. As Robert Eadon Leader in his *Reminiscences of Sheffield* asserts,

> "…the booksellers kept in stock works that only specialists among their successors would think of storing" [6].

This did, however, have a beneficial impact on the education of generations of offspring of Sheffield booksellers. Leader explains when discussing the life of John Pye Smith, a future Professor of Theology at Homerton College and the son of the bookseller John Smith, a neighbour of Thomas Cawthorn on Angel Street, who had a particular interest in theological texts:

> "It was from these deep sources that his son, young John Pye Smith, profiting by their unsaleable character, got the foundation of his profound learning at a time when most boys are playing or reading tales" [7].

Indeed, Leader goes on to describe the stocks of unsaleable books held by some of the Sheffield booksellers:

> "The bookseller regarded them with the affection due to old friends, but they were not, from a commercial point of view, a paying speculation: and some of them to this day enrich the libraries of his descendants. Such deductions as may be derived from the fact that this kind were on sale in a provincial town must therefore, be discounted by the knowledge that they soared far above the heads of such book-buyers as existed among the public" [8].

This was the environment in which the young James Cawthorn was raised. As the eldest son, he would no doubt have been left to "mind the shop" whilst his father attended to his various business interests in and around the city. Given the unlikeliness of actually having any customers, Cawthorn would have had ample time to read through his father's library of books at his leisure. Soon he was beginning to write more accomplished pieces of his own and his first published poem, *Meditation on the Power of God*, appeared anonymously in the *Gentleman's Magazine* in September 1735 [9]. Quite apart from the fact that a prominent London magazine felt the poem to be worthy of publication, it is also a remarkable subject for a fifteen-year-old to have the confidence to tackle. Like much of Cawthorn's poetry, this work takes its inspiration from Alexander Pope, and in particular, his *Essay on Man*[10]. Much of Pope's work, like Haywood's, was published by both Roberts and Henry Woodfall.

Like James Roberts, Henry Woodfall also worked with a range of different booksellers. In particular, he printed a number of works for the partnership of Arthur Bettesworth and Charles Hitch – for example, another book by Eliza Haywood, *Secret Histories, Novels and Poems*, which was printed in 1732 [11]. It may be through Woodfall that James Cawthorn first became acquainted with Charles Hitch, a bookseller with whom he would establish a life-long friendship and whom he remembered in his will, leaving money to his "worthy friend" [12] and his wife for them to purchase "a ring or some other memorial"[13] by which to remember him. Bettesworth and Hitch were amongst the first booksellers to recognise the talents of Samuel Johnson, publishing his translation of *A Voyage to Abyssinia by Father Jerome Lobo*, a Portuguese Jesuit in 1735 [14]. Hitch later formed a partnership with seven other prominent London booksellers to fund Johnson's seminal *Dictionary of the English Language* which was eventually published in 1755[15], the year before the Cawthorn Library was built.

In 1738 Cawthorn left Sheffield and moved to Cambridge where on the 8th July he matriculated at Clare Hall, Cambridge University [16]. His career as a university student, however, appears to have been short-lived for there is no record of him actually graduating. The year 1738 was also, coincidentally, the year in which Samuel Johnson's first widely acclaimed work *London – A Poem* was published by the printer Robert Dodsley [17]. It was not long before Cawthorn was also discovering the attractions of London for himself when he moved to the capital and took up employment as a teacher at the Soho Academy.

Hence it is that at this early point in his life, Cawthorn already knows, and is known to the London bookselling and printing community.

Cawthorn worked at the Soho Academy until 1743 and his association with the London bookselling and printing community becomes ever more apparent after he left in order to become Headmaster of Tonbridge School. An appreciation of the significance of this association becomes clear through an analysis of the "School Lists" or Register of Pupils at Tonbridge over the years.

The School Lists

There are a number of sources of information in respect of the school registers for Tonbridge, but the most complete source for the period in question is undoubtedly W.G.

Hart's *The Register of Tonbridge School from 1553 to 1820,* published by Rivington's in 1935.

Hart's compendium provides not only the lists of names of boys who were at the school but also gives a description of the character and composition of the register:

> It is evident that during the eighteenth century – at any rate from the beginning of Mr Spencer's Head Mastership – the School aimed at being, and in fact was, of a distinctly aristocratic character. So far as it is possible to identify and to trace their origin, they are almost all the sons of people in good social position – country gentleman, army officers, barristers, clergymen, and the like – very rarely is it that one finds the son of a tradesman among them.[18]

In so far as it goes, this description is reasonably fair and when Cawthorn became headmaster, the boys on the school register could typically be divided into three broad categories:

Local Boys – These boys accounted for a significant contingent of boys on the school register and as Hart observes,

> "… appear to have been drawn to a large extent from the county families of Kent and Sussex. The Bathursts, the Boys, the Childrens, the Dalysons, the Husseys, the Lades, the Styles, the Woodgates and others whose names appear in the

lists – in some cases for four, five, and even more generations."[19]

To Hart's list of local boys can also be added the names of the Walters and the Wellers, amongst many others from in and around Tonbridge. The Austen family also first appears in the lists when Henry Austen joined the school in 1734 – although some "Austines" are recorded a century earlier.

London Boys – Given its proximity to London, the school also attracted a large contingent of boys from the capital. These boys were often, but not exclusively, the sons of families connected in one way or another to the Skinners' Company; for example:

> Charles Asgill (O.T. 1724-26), the son of a London merchant who followed his father into business and also became a member of the Skinners' Company where he was appointed Master in 1748. He went on to become Lord Mayor of London 1757-58.

> John Barnardiston (O.T. 1728-37) was another London boy. The son of a barrister, George Barnardiston of Middle Temple, John matriculated at Corpus Christi College, Cambridge in 1737 where he was eventually appointed Master from 1764 until his death in 1778.

Empire Boys – As the British Empire expanded in the eighteenth century a growing number of families left the British Isles in order to seek their fame and fortune in the new overseas territories. It was quite common, however, for this diaspora of families to send their sons back to Britain for their formal education. In the case of Tonbridge School, the Caribbean was particularly well represented in the school lists.

Families such as the Byams and the Warners of Antigua, the Alleynes of Barbados and the Gordons of Jamaica.

Many of these boys later returned to the West Indies where they established successful careers in both business and public service.

Although not formally categorised as such, these three groups are each, nevertheless, acknowledged and described by Hart. What Hart does not recognise however, is that under Cawthorn's tenure as headmaster a fourth and very distinctive group emerges – the sons of booksellers.

The Literary Connection

These sons of booksellers and publishers were from mainly London-based families as London was the principle centre of publishing in England during this period. The first of these "Literary Boys" appeared fairly early during Cawthorn's tenure but the trend accelerated once the library was built.

Literary Boys – a number of prominent publishing and bookselling families began to send their sons to be educated by Cawthorn at Tonbridge, including:

The Hitch family – Cawthorn's "worthy friend" Charles Hitch – who became Master of the Stationers' Company in 1758 - sent his eldest son, also called Charles (O.T. 1748-53), to be educated at Tonbridge very early during Cawthorn's tenure as headmaster. His second son, Paul Hitch (O.T. 1753-63), followed his brother and became Head Boy in 1763 under Cawthorn's successor, The Rev. Johnson Towers.

The Woodfall family – Henry Woodfall, the publisher for Thomas Cawthorn's business partner George Steer, was succeeded as head of the family's publishing company by his son, also called Henry. Henry Woodfall Junior, who was a few years older than James Cawthorn, married Mary Sampson and the couple had three sons and a daughter. The eldest son, Henry Sampson Woodfall, was educated at St Paul's, but his younger brother, the celebrated parliamentary reporter William Woodfall (O.T. 1756 -60), also known as "Memory Woodfall", joined Tonbridge in the same year that Cawthorn's library was built. The youngest son, Charles Woodfall (O.T. 1760 -61), followed his brother to Tonbridge.

The Rivington family – the Rivingtons were one of the most celebrated London publishing families of the eighteenth century, although their focus on particularly religious texts began to fall out of favour during the period which became known as the "Enlightenment" era. Francis Rivington (O.T. 1757-59) joined Tonbridge School shortly after Cawthorn's library was built and this was the beginning of a long association between Tonbridge and the Rivingtons. Septimus Rivington, great-nephew of Francis, would go on to write *The History of Tonbridge School from it Foundation in 1533 to The Present Day* first published in 1869 and the Rivingtons were also the publishers of W.G. Hart's *Tonbridge School Register* in 1935.

These were only some of the literary families who sent their sons to be educated by Cawthorn at Tonbridge, and the significance of the establishment and increasing presence of this literary connection during his tenure as headmaster cannot be underestimated. His relationship with the bookseller and publishing community is one that Cawthorn took very seriously and nurtured particularly carefully. This was not always easy and required careful tact and diplomacy in order to successfully appeal to as wide a range of literary families as possible. In order to do this, Cawthorn had to avoid being drawn into some of the disputes which arose periodically amongst this competitive, opinionated and fractious community. For a man who was well-known amongst this community and who had from a very early age been "a keen observer of men and manners" and quick to put his thoughts and opinions into print, a mature self-discipline was essential. The attraction of the bookseller and literary community to a bibliophile headmaster trying to establish and develop a school library was obvious, but the path that Cawthorn had to tread in order to maintain a broad appeal to this particular constituency was not always an easy one.

Treading a delicate path

The delicate path that Cawthorn had to tread is best illustrated by an episode which occurred in 1749 when the eminent writer Henry Fielding published what is often regarded as his greatest book – *The History of Tom Jones - A Foundling*. The book, as its title suggests, tells the story of an illegitimate boy, Tom Jones, who is abandoned before being adopted and raised by a kind and wealthy country squire. It is set against the background of the Jacobite uprising of 1745 and explores numerous issues of the day including prostitution and sexual promiscuity. Often described as one of the first novels, the book offers what is, at times, a biting social commentary on morals and double standards prevalent at the time. Although it was an instant sensation and a huge commercial success, the book also caused widespread outrage and received as much criticism as praise at the time of its publication, with Samuel Johnson, for example, claiming that he "scarcely knows a more corrupt work"[20].

One reader, however, was in no doubt whatsoever about the merits of the book and wrote an open letter to the *Gentleman's Magazine* with undisguised poetical praise for Fielding's brilliance:

"To Henry Fielding, Esq – on reading his inimitable History of Tom Jones:

'Long thro' the mimic scenes of motley life,
Neglected Nature lost th' unequal strife,
Studious to show, in mad fantastic shape,
Each grinning gesture of his kindred ape,
Man lost the name: while each in artful dress,
Appear'd still something more or something less,
Virtue and vice, unmix'd, in fancy stood,
And all were vilely bad, or greatly good;
Eternal distance ever made to keep,
Exciting horror, or promoting sleep:
Sick of her fools, great Nature broke the jest,
And Truth held out each character to test,
When Genius spoke; Let Fielding take the pen!
Life dropt her mask, and all mankind were men."[21]

The letter appeared in August 1749 and although it was signed "THO. CAWTHORN"[22], it was immediately attributed to James Cawthorn, which given its style and content, is quite understandable. It was also common practice for letter writers of the day to use a pseudonym when writing about particularly contentious subjects, although in this case the author's chosen disguise appears to be pretty thin. The attribution, however, was not entirely welcome and, in a short time, proved to be uncomfortable for Cawthorn.

Henry Fielding was a divisive figure in the literary world and a few years earlier had been involved in a very public spat with another writer, Samuel Richardson, who prior to taking up his pen was a well-known and popular printer and bookseller in his own right. Richardson had been commissioned in 1739 by the publishers Charles

Rivington and John Osborn to write a book in the form of a series of letters, designed to offer guidance to readers on a range of moral issues [23]. In the process of doing so he had the idea for another book, which was published in 1740 under the title *Pamela: or Virtue Rewarded* [24]. The book, which was Richardson's first novel, told the story of its heroine Pamela Andrews, a beautiful maidservant who protects her virtue against the advances of unwelcome suitors and is eventually rewarded with an advantageous proposal of marriage. The book was immediately popular with a wide audience and also enjoyed significant commercial success. Some readers, however, found it to be far too pious and patronising and the characters unrealistically one dimensional – either very vilely bad or too greatly good. The book prompted a notable backlash, with Cawthorn's favourite female satirist Eliza Haywood publishing *The Anti-Pamela; or Feign'd Innocence Detected* [25] in 1741 and, most famously, in the same year Fielding joined the fray with *An Apology for the Life of Mrs Shamela Andrews,* published under the pseudonym of Mr Conny Keyber [26], which mercilessly parodied Richardson's book. Cawthorn had to tread with care. Richardson was a friend of Henry Woodfall and had also been given a contract by the Speaker of the House of Commons, Arthur Onslow – one of Martin Clare's patrons – to publish parliamentary journals [27]. He was clearly popular amongst Cawthorn's social circle in London and furthermore, one of Richardson's publishers for Pamela had been Charles Hitch who in 1745 had printed Cawthorn's *Sermon Preached before the Worshipful Burgesses of Westminster* [28]. In 1748 he had also sent his eldest son, Charles, to Tonbridge – one of the first of the "Literary Boys" to enrol at the school.

Given Fielding's controversial reputation amongst the bookseller community and Cawthorn's desire to cultivate his literary connections, it was not wise for the Headmaster of Tonbridge School to be seen to be taking sides in what appeared to be another outbreak of hostilities amongst the literati. Somewhat prudently therefore, the following disclaimer appeared in the *Gentleman's Magazine* in October 1749:

> "N.B. The verses to Henry Fielding, Esq; P371 signed Tho. Cawthorn were not written by the Master of Tunbridge School" [29].

It is not unreasonable to view this episode in Cawthorn's life through the narrow perspective of his relationship with the bookseller community of London as it clearly illustrates the delicate path he had to tread.

Further Considerations

However, there are, of course, a number of other aspects of the story which are also worthy of consideration. Fielding's *Tom Jones* did not only excite equal measures of love and loathing amongst the London booksellers. Despite its huge popularity it was nevertheless a controversial book and was condemned not only by Samuel Johnson for its corrupting influence on the book-reading public. This was not necessarily the type of publication that the parents of

Tonbridge boys of the time would expect to see their sons' headmaster's name associated with in the literary press of the day. As Hart describes in the School Register, the school from the time of Cawthorn's predecessor, Richard Spencer, "aimed at being, and in fact was of a distinctly aristocratic character"[30], with almost all of the boys "the sons of people in good social position" [31] and "the School was in high repute with the classes who then ruled England and her colonies" [32]. Once again Cawthorn had to be careful. His patrons expected an essentially classical education for their sons, which they believed would more than adequately equip them for the lives they were destined to lead. There was no place in the schoolroom for base novels containing biting social commentary which satirised the often hypocritical standards of the day and the headmaster of a school such as Tonbridge should not be legitimising such a book by extolling its virtues in print. It was not only in his attempts to appeal to the London bookselling and publishing community that Cawthorn had to avoid becoming embroiled in literary controversies and feuds of the day; he had also to be careful that he did not alienate his core constituency who had traditionally chosen Tonbridge School for their sons' education.

The disclaimer published by Cawthorn in the October 1749 edition of the *Gentleman's Magazine* served its purpose and the debate and controversy moved on with no further reference to the supposed views of Tonbridge School's headmaster.

It is nevertheless interesting to speculate as to how accurate the original attribution may have been in identifying James Cawthorn as the author of the original verse. The wording is intriguing in this regard: – "the verses... signed Tho. Cawthorn were not written by the Master of Tunbridge..." So who did write them? Who was Thomas Cawthorn and is the phrase "not written by" the equivalent of claiming "not composed by"? The Thomas Cawthorn in question may well have been Cawthorn's brother who, born in 1723, was four years younger than James. Thomas had followed his older brother to Sheffield Grammar School where it was noted "penmanship was taught as a fine art"[33] before also moving to London where in 1745, perhaps with the help of his older brother, he had entered into the Freedom of the Skinners' Company[34]. James and Thomas were close and it is quite possible that what actually happened is that James, fully aware of the potential outcry that would result from such public praise of Henry Fielding's *Tom Jones*, actually solicited his brother to pen a poem which James had in fact composed.

Whatever the true story behind the open letter to Henry Fielding in the *Gentleman's Magazine* of 1749, it nevertheless served as a warning to James Cawthorn about the dangers and pitfalls of becoming publicly involved with the eighteenth century literati. On the one hand, Cawthorn was clearly at home amongst the booksellers and publishers of London. His relationship with this community also offered opportunities for the bibliophile headmaster in helping to fulfil his dream of establishing once and for all a purpose-built library at Tonbridge. On the other hand however, he had learnt that in order to avoid alienating potential patrons of his school – both amongst its traditional constituency and also amongst the bookselling and publishing community with whom the headmaster was trying to develop his relationships – he needed to avoid becoming publicly embroiled in the periodic disputes, rivalries and petty feuds that were a near constant feature of the eighteenth century London literary scene.

Discretion is a Virtue

This was clearly a lesson which Cawthorn was quick to learn and his name does not appear publically again in the context of the literary scene in London with its attendant and periodic feuds. This is not, however, to suggest that he was not still actively engaged within the bookselling and publishing world and evidence of his continuing involvement is not hard to find. For example, in the mid 1750s, around the time that the first school library was under construction at Tonbridge, the celebrated publisher Robert Dodsley was in something of an ongoing stand-off with the theatre owner and playwright David Garrick.

Dodsley, whose shop at the sign of Tully's Head in Pall Mall also features in one of Cawthorn's poem's [35], had an unpromising start in life in which he spent some time working as a footman in London. During this time, however, he wrote some notable poetry which brought him to the attention of some of the key literary figures of the day. Cawthorn's favourite poet Alexander Pope, in particular helped Dodsley to establish himself as a bookseller and publisher, a business in which he very quickly established himself in a position of some repute. His publication of Samuel Johnson's *London – A Poem* in 1738 was a seminal moment in the lives of both men. Despite his success in producing other people's work, Dodsley continued to write on his own account throughout his life, not only in the form of poetry but also as a playwright. He enjoyed considerable success with his works on the stage and in the mid 1750s embarked upon a new project when he started work on a tragedy based upon the story of Cleone, which he borrowed from the legend of St Genevieve [36]. His intention, apparently, at the outset of this project was that his *Tragedy of Cleone* was to be performed at the leading playhouse of the day, David Garrick's Drury Lane Theatre. Unfortunately, Garrick rejected the play time and again despite constant revisions by Dodsley. Undeterred, Dodsley drew upon the support of a number of his literary friends to help with his revisions which continued over a number of years, such that,

> "In the long incubation of Cleone, while holding tenaciously to his initial conception of plot and characterisations, he had made extensive use of the critiques of friends – especially Berenger, Graves, Hawksworth and Shenstone" [37].

To this list can also be added James Cawthorn's name when in early 1757, Dodsley sent Cawthorn a copy of the tragedy and sought his advice on his latest draft. Cawthorn responded to the request in the form of a letter which he sent to Dodsley via the reliable hands of Charles Hitch. Although Cawthorn's letter is now unfortunately lost, an indication of its contents and hence Cawthorn's thoughts on the script is apparent in a reply sent to Cawthorn from Dodsley in April of 1757. It is clear from Dodsley's letter that Cawthorn had read the script in detail and had offered his advice:

> "Dear Sir,
> My friend Mr Hitch has been so kind as to shew me your candid and judicious remarks on my Tragedy of Cleone. It plainly appears from your letter that you have not thought it unworthy of being read with attention, and your general approbation of it, after such a perusal, gives me a very sensible pleasure" [38].

Dodsley proceeded to address a number of points which Cawthorn had clearly raised in which he had felt compelled to criticise the work including both its overall style and some specific characterisations. It is also clear from his letter that he wished to pursue the matter further with Cawthorn;

> "... I am really more oblig'd to you for your criticisms than your commendations, and hope when you come to town I may reap the benefit of your minutest objection" [39].

He continues later in the letter:

> "... In this endeavour I doubtless may have fail'd in many places, and when we meet shall be very glad to have them pointed out by so good a judge" [40].

Although there is no surviving historical record to confirm that a subsequent meeting took place between the two men, there is no reason from the tone of the letter to suppose otherwise.

Dodsley persevered with his revisions to *Cleone* but was unable to persuade Garrick to perform the play at his Drury Lane theatre and in the end it opened at John Rich's less fashionable Covent Garden venue. Garrick, however, was determined to see the play fail and scheduled the opening night of his latest production, *Busy Body,* to open on the same evening. The literati of London were once again split and highly partisan reviews of both shows subsequently appeared in the journals of the day. Notably however, despite Cawthorn's modest contribution to the saga, his name did not appear publicly in the ensuing battle between the literati. He had clearly learnt his lesson.

A Headmaster of Considerable Reputation

It is not surprising that W. G. Hart observes that,

> "Among literary people of the eighteenth century Mr Cawthorn was a man of considerable reputation" [41].

It is clear that by the time the first Tonbridge School library was built in 1756 James Cawthorn was held in high esteem by the booksellers and publishers of London. They sent their sons to be taught by him at Tonbridge School and also sought his opinion on their own literary works. The symbiotic attraction of a school with only a modest collection of books, a bibliophile headmaster with a zealous commitment to firmly establish a school library, and the families of prominent booksellers is quite obvious. However, for the relationship to work to its full advantage something else was needed: a catalyst of sorts, to both fund and encourage a regular supply of the latest texts from the booksellers to the library.

For this catalyst Cawthorn turned to another important book – the school rules.

CHAPTER SIX

From Rule Books to School Books

The original rules for the government of Tonbridge School are laid out in the statues written at the formation of the school in the sixteenth century. These, however, only cover such matters as the salary to be paid to the Master and the requirements needed by a boy in order to be accepted into the school. They do not cover the day-to-day running of the school by the Master and his assistants and do not therefore cover the rules and punishments a boy could expect to find on admittance into Tonbridge. These, to a large extent, were left to the discretion of individual headmasters; and unfortunately, the Tonbridge School rule book for Cawthorn's time as headmaster no longer exists. However, it is not unreasonable to assume that it was in large part based upon the rule book of his previous school, the Soho Academy.

Rules and Orders

The *Rules and Orders for the Government of the Academy in Soho Square, London* [1] is a remarkable book. It was written by Martin Clare, proprietor and headmaster of the Academy and his deputy, the Rev. Cuthbert Barwis. There is no publication date for the book recorded at the British Library, but Nicholas Hans dates its publication quite reasonably as being between 1744 and 1751. The way in which he reaches this conclusion is very straightforward, for as he points out, Barwis is styled MA on the title page and therefore as,

"… Martin Clare died in 1751 and Barwis received M.A. in 1744, the publication of the 'Rules' was made between these two dates" [2].

These dates are, of course, very significant because they clearly suggest that the publication of the Soho Academy's rule book was a direct response to the "curious" and unfortunate death of Thomas Ricketts in 1743. Ricketts' death was a defining moment for the Academy and the apparent lack of discipline at the school was cruelly exposed as a result. The publication of the rule book appears to have been a direct attempt to counter the negative publicity to which the school was exposed and was part of its attempts at public rehabilitation after this appalling incident.

Martin Clare had not only been Cawthorn's employer before he became Headmaster of Tonbridge, but after James' marriage to Mary Clare on the 14th November 1742 [3] he had also become his father-in-law. Similarly, Cuthbert Barwis became Cawthorn's brother-in-law after his marriage to Martin Clare's other daughter, Anne Clare, in 1745. In addition to his position at the Soho Academy, Martin

Clare was elected a Fellow of the Royal Society on the 27th March 1735 and became an avid subscriber to the Society's *Philosophical Transactions*, a periodical which he ensured occupied a prominent place amongst the publications owned by his son-in-law's school as observed by Rivington in his *History of Tonbridge School* when he notes:

> "There is an inscription in the first volume of the Philosophical Transactions in the School Library at Tonbridge... Martinus Clare, A.M., F.R.S. Dono dedit. Anno 1745" [4].

It is highly likely therefore that Martin Clare would also share with his son-in-law his views on how a good school should be run. Cawthorn in turn would have been acutely aware of his own guilt by association in respect of the death of Thomas Ricketts after the reception he received from parents of boys at Tonbridge to his appointment as headmaster. Ricketts' death was a traumatic and defining moment in the history of the Soho Academy and Cawthorn would no doubt have read the ensuing publicity and recognised the potentially catastrophic impact such an incident could have on a school and its reputation. The beneficial opportunity that the adoption of his in-law's publication therefore offered him in terms of demonstrating a clear and objective commitment to a sound disciplinary regime is quite obvious. It is also fair to say that "*Rules and Orders...*" was a publication which perfectly suited Cawthorn's requirements when it came to raising funds to purchase books for his school library.

The curious case of the schoolboy who was killed in

an argument over a slice of cake would play an important part in the development of the Cawthorn Library at Tonbridge School.

Omissions, Commissions and Capital Offences

The stated purpose of *Rules and Orders for the Government of the Academy in Soho Square, London* was to ensure that "the Scholar may be apprised of the Discipline" [5] in the school, and the introduction goes on to state that "it is expected that the Scholar should in all Respects conform to what is thus given" [6].

The rule book lists a series of rules and regulations and outlines the penalties for scholars who do not "conform".

The first list concerns "Petty Omissions" such as:

"Entering or Leaving the Schools without showing the due and usual respect"

"Not rising, in Decency, when the Principal Masters or Strangers (Servants excepted) first enter the school"

"Not proceeding in any Lesson, upon the Word"

"Not giving a tolerable Account of a Publick Lecture" [7]

This list is followed by a second list concerning "Petty Commissions", including such as:

> "Loitering or illiberal Language or Behaviour in the Way to and from School"
>
> "Dirtiness in Person or in Clothes"
>
> "Eating in Time of Study"
>
> "Coming within a Quarter of an Hour too late by the School Dial"
>
> "Refusing another a Passage when desired"
>
> "Displacing another's Books or Implements, or making Use of them without the Owner's Licence"
>
> "Being noted for Clamour, Unquietness or Petulance in the Monitor's Bill" [8]

The book outlines the punishment for breaking each and any of the above rules:

> "The Penalty to each of the Faults above is one eighth of a Penny, or proportionate Punishment"[9]

The book then turns to "Grand Omissions", where both the crimes and the penalties become more onerous, such as:

> "Inattention to Reading the Holy Scripture, Misbehaviour in Time of Prayer, and not Reading the Morning Psalms with Sobriety and Devotion" [10]

The punishment in this case is – "Discretionary"! [11]

Similarly, serious tardiness also attracts a more severe punishment in so far as:

> "Coming from a Quarter to Half an Hour after the appointed Time" [12]

This results in a fine of a "Half-Penny".

In the case of "Grand Commissions" the punishments increase further:

> "Buying, Selling or Gaming in School-time" [13]

This results in a fine of "One Penny", as does:

> "Being found out of School in the Hours of Study, without sufficient Leave from the Masters or some of their Assistants" [14]

In the case of damage to school property the punishment is determined by the nature of the crime, such that:

> "Penalty on a Voluntary Confession" is "only making the damage good". However, "… if it be concealed purposely, the Penalty is – one Penny besides" [15].

Finally, the rule book covers the most serious misdemeanours, known as "Capital Offences" where, most likely for the avoidance of doubt, the punishment is described before the rules are listed:

"The Penalty to these is – Whipping" [16]

The most serious capital offences are listed first and printed in capital letters in order to emphasis their seriousness:

"LYING. THEFT. REBELLION. SWEARING or CURSING. REVILING or PROVOCATION. IMMODEST SPEECH. TRUANTING. STRIKING (ie: fighting) in Schools and The AGRESSOR in a Quarrel out of Schools" [17]

Other "Capital Offences" included, unsurprisingly:

"Wilful and Extraordinary Abuse of Books and School Implements" [18]

And extreme tardiness such as:

"Coming more than half an Hour too late without sufficient Warrant" [19]

In reality, however, the punishment for a capital offence was open to negotiation and a whipping could usually be avoided on payment of a fine of sufficient magnitude to match the scale of the alleged misdemeanour. Two "monitors" appointed for the task, kept a record of every boy's list of offences and each term's account for fines incurred had to be settled in the first week of the following term [20].

It is no exaggeration to say that a young man who did

not behave impeccably and apply himself diligently to his lessons could soon find he had accrued a very substantial "extras bill" to be added to his tuition fees. From the school's perspective, the monies raised as a result of boys' names being entered in the monitors' diaries represented a form of additional revenue which varied in direct proportion to the extent and manner in which discipline was administered. The behaviour of boys, both individually and collectively, obviously influenced the number of times that names were entered into the monitors' books and fines levied. So too, however, did the behaviour of the Masters. The application of the rules was open to significant interpretation and the amount of revenue raised as a result of the extent to which fines were levied, was in large part determined by the perceived disciplinary character of the Master.

The school rules were written in such a way that a severe disciplinarian would most likely raise considerably more money through a liberal use of the rule book, than would a more liberal Master with a somewhat more laissez-faire approach to controlling classroom behaviour.

Use of Funds raised from Disciplinary Fines

The Soho Academy's *Rules and Orders…* goes on to explain how the Masters of the Academy would apply the funds raised each term from the admission of punishments, "… to the Advantage of the Pupils" [21]. Expenditure was apportioned in the following order:

> Boys who perform well during the year will be "… intitled to partake of a Collation and a Country-Dance" [22]

Remaining funds were then divided as follows:

> Funds were "… applied to recompense the more conspicuous for Diligence in the Ordinary Exercises, and to reward such as excel in the weekly school contests" [23]

> "… the remainder shall be laid out for Books, Instruments and proper Assistances to be kept as a fixt Library… " [24]

The Soho Academy was thus able to utilise a source of revenue which was supplementary to the income it received from tuition fees. This income stream was used to broaden the curriculum for boys at the school whilst also rewarding academic excellence. In addition, however, funds were also used to establish and expand the school's library. This was in turn a feature of the Academy which Martin Clare highlighted when promoting the attractions of his school to prospective patrons and as Nicholas Hans points out, "The Academy had a select library" [25]. Clare was a gifted educationalist and an astute businessman who had realised the growing importance of eighteenth century schools establishing and developing their own recognisable school libraries. His son-in-law learnt much from the example of his father-in-law.

Discipline at Tonbridge

It is not difficult to envisage how Cawthorn would have adopted a similar "Rules and Orders" book for use at Tonbridge. It offered him not only an opportunity to demonstrate a clear commitment to a sound disciplinary regime, which in itself was useful after the inauspicious start to his term of office, but also offered the potential to raise significant additional revenue which need not be under the control of the Skinners' Company. The school rule book offered Cawthorn a means by which he could raise funds for books with which to develop the school's library collection.

It is also the case that the aristocratic composition of the school register as described by Hart did indeed include a majority of boys from families with a "good social position"[26], many of whom were well placed to contribute to the "monitors' list". For example, a young Sampson Gideon (O.T. 1752-60), who was the only son of one of the most successful and influential financiers of the eighteenth century, would have been of particular interest to the fundraising crusade of the bibliophile, and notably disciplinarian, headmaster.

The young Gideon's father, also called Sampson, had been a very active and successful trader in the shares of the South Sea Company during the South Sea Bubble of 1720-1[27] and whilst making himself a fortune, had earned the moniker of "the great oracle and leader of Jonathan's Coffee House in Exchange Alley" [28], the forerunner of the London Stock Exchange. In the 1730-40s his advice had been invaluable to both Walpole and Pelham in raising funds to finance wars against Spain and her allies, from the War of Jenkin's Ear through to the War of the Austrian Succession and included making his estates available to the government in order to thwart the advance of Bonny Prince Charlie's Jacobites during "The Forty-Five".

Sampson Jnr entered Tonbridge School in 1752, four years before Cawthorn's library was built. The year in which the construction of the library took place, 1756, also marked the outbreak of the Seven Years War, when Gideon Snr was again called upon to help fund Britain's war effort. Although enjoying some early successes on the battlefield, the war soon turned against Britain and her allies and by the time of the Skinners' Company visitation to Tonbridge in May 1759, the Kent countryside was garrisoned with thousands of troops as Britain prepared to face the very real threat of a French invasion. The mood of the moment was reflected in Cawthorn's poetry written for that year's visitation and recited by the Head Boy, James Thurston – *Verses Occasioned by the Victory of Rossbach* [29]. The poetry harked back to the victory early in the war, in November 1757, of Britain's ally, Frederick the Great, over a vastly superior combined force of French and Austrians in Saxony, and is amongst Cawthorn's most stirring verse:

"Awake, Voltaire! With warmth, with rapture raise
Th' applauding Poean, and the song of praise
Again thy Fred'ric mounts the victor's car,
Again he thunders in the front of war;
Back to the desert flies the routed Gaul,
And proud Vienna shakes from wall to wall…' [30]

It would, however, take more than fine words to turn the tide of war. What was needed was victory on the battlefield and this would require ever more expensive military operations, all of which needed funding. Once again the government turned to Sampson Gideon and once again he, almost single-handedly, raised the required finance which enabled Britain's forces to remain in the field and turned 1759 into the Year of Victories; the expulsion of the French from North America with the fall of Quebec City after the Battle of the Plain of Abraham; the relief of the French Siege of Madras in India; the major allied victory in Europe at the Battle of Minden and the Royal Navy assuming mastery of the seas after the Battle of Quiberon Bay.

Horace Walpole reflecting on the annus miribalis, remarked, "Our bells are worn threadbare with ringing for victories" [31], and a grateful government was eager to honour the financier whose tireless efforts had financially underwritten the military achievements. It was proposed that a baronetcy should be awarded but unfortunately, under the constitution, this was impossible on account of Gideon being a Jew. He had, however, married a member of the Church of England, Elizabeth Erwell, and their children had all been raised as Christians. As such, it was decided to award the title to his son, Sampson Gideon Jnr, and the young Tonbridge schoolboy was informed accordingly in a letter he received from his father:

"DEAR SAMPSON,
The King has been pleased to order his letters patent to promote you to the dignity of a baronet;

it is the lowest hereditary honour but the first step. I have hopes that by your own merit you will go higher; I shall otherwise wish his majesty had not been so generous... Behave, my dear boy, as you have hitherto done towards your master, schoolfellows and everybody...

Your affectionate father
SAMPSON GIDEON

Postscript – Show this with our compliments to Mr. Cawthorne, then keep it clean till you come home."[32]

Gideon Snr and James Cawthorn were obviously known to each other and given the length of time the young Sampson was at Tonbridge, there was undoubtedly a mutual respect between his father and his headmaster. It was also, however, a relationship which the fundraising disciplinarian headmaster could use to good effect in terms of his own revenue raising efforts, required in order to stock his newly built library. It was not only in the service of his country that Sampson Gideon proved a notable benefactor, for the Tonbridge School library also benefitted in no small measure from his financial acumen. Gideon Snr could well afford any fines his son may accrue in the monitors' book and as such it is highly likely that the young Gideon was on the receiving end of Cawthorn's perceived disciplinary reign of terror.

Septimus Rivington alludes to the possibility that Sampson Gideon's name may indeed have been a familiar entry in the book of fines, kept by the likes of George

Austen during his time as Usher, and Cawthorn's other monitors, for he states when discussing the young man's relationship with Cawthorn:

"... he never mentioned his Master's name without trepidation... "[33]

Such was the manner in which Cawthorn exploited the "distinctly aristocratic"[34] nature of much of the Tonbridge School register. A highly original and targeted use of the school's rule book ensured a steady supply of funds which were not in any way under the control of the Skinners' Company. Funds which could be raised on a scale which was in direct proportion to the perceived disciplinary character of the headmaster. It is hardly surprising that certain boys on the school lists lived in "trepidation" of their stern, disciplinarian master. However hard they tried to please their teacher, it was nevertheless inevitable that their efforts would never be enough to prevent their names being entered in the monitors' lists.

Sense and Sensibility

Not every boy, however, would find their name entered onto the monitors' lists. Cawthorn may well have acquired a reputation as a severe disciplinarian as a result of his liberal interpretation and use of the school's rule book, but it is also the case that he is reported as being "ever ready to applaud merit" [35]. This seems to have been the case from the very earliest days of his tenure as headmaster, when to some extent the pressure on him to demonstrate a firm disciplinary grip was at its most extreme given the unfortunate newspaper reports about the lack of discipline at his previous school and the controversial nature of his appointment as Headmaster of Tonbridge.

George Austen (O.T. 1741-47), for example, when he was a pupil at the school at the time of Cawthorn's appointment, seems to have escaped entry into the monitors' book. Indeed, he appears to have positively thrived under the headmaster's apparently severe regime. According to David Nokes in his account of Austen's childhood:

> "George Austen remembered Tonbridge School with a good deal of affection. It was there he had learnt to thrive under the patient discipline and sound instruction of his masters" [36].

For a poor orphan, dependent upon the goodwill of a benevolent uncle to fund his schooling, the avoidance of an unnecessary addition to his fees was a matter of some importance. Whilst Austen's obvious work ethic and good behaviour no doubt helped in this regard, it would also have been the case that he was not a natural target for the focused crusade of his despotic master.

Clearly a boy's "social position" and family background had a significant influence on his disciplinary experience whilst at Tonbridge under Cawthorn. George Austen was undoubtedly a bright and able pupil, but it was also the case that he was a young boy whose family background had resulted in him living in somewhat reduced circumstances and dependent upon the benevolence of his relatives. Cawthorn was aware of this distinction and appears to have treated the young Austen with kindness, patience and tolerance. His name did not need to enter the monitors' book and had it done so, he may well have experienced a degree of unwelcome and unhelpful chastisement from his uncles into whose guardianship he had been placed after the death of his father. Common sense and sensitivity appear to have been the defining characteristics of Cawthorn's treatment of Austen during his time as a pupil at Tonbridge.

On the other hand, the somewhat less intellectually able but rather more financially privileged young men such as Sampson Gideon appear to have had a markedly more testing experience under Cawthorn's tuition. These boys undoubtedly received the essentially classical education their parents were expecting, but were taught in an environment where their failings and inadequacies were mercilessly exposed and exploited. Cawthorn was a headmaster on a crusade; a mission to succeed where his predecessors had failed, in finally and firmly establishing a clearly recognisable school library at Tonbridge School and the "distinctly aristocratic" school roll offered an attractive revenue generating opportunity for a headmaster with a new school library to stock.

The more often that discipline was imposed, the more money was raised in the form of fines and penalties. It did, however, pay for the disciplinarian headmaster's bark to be worse than his bite – his objective was to raise funds for his library rather than to whip his charges into submission. Contributions to the school monitors were likely to be more common than the administration of corporal punishment.

The Use of Funds

The way in which Cawthorn would apply the funds "… for the advantage of the pupils" is also easy to imagine and was most likely in principle, the same as at the Soho Academy, only in reverse order:

Monies would be applied first of all in buying books for the "… fixt library".

There was, however, little need to "recompense the more conspicuous for diligence… and to reward such as excel" because this role at Tonbridge was performed by the Skinners' Company at the annual visitation. During this annual inspection of the school, an examiner appointed by the Skinners would test the six most able pupils, selected by the headmaster and if they "… severally aquitted themselves with reputation and credit", then "…. to each (was) delivered a Silver Pen quill gift" [37].

Whilst, in order to maintain the headmaster's reputation as "harsh in school matters" [38], it is highly unlikely that anything would be left over for a "… Collation and… Country Dance".

In practice therefore, the monies raised through the imaginative and targeted use of the school rule book were most likely used exclusively for the development of the Cawthorn Library collection.

The Story behind the myths

Although in reality, there were most likely a number of ways in which Cawthorn raised the funds needed to stock his library, his highly original use of the school rule book played a significant role.

So it came about that James Cawthorn turned the adversity occasioned by the curious case of the schoolboy who was killed in an argument over a slice of cake at the Soho Academy in London, to the advantage of Tonbridge School, and the development of the school library.

Through a judicious use of the school's rule book and the targeted imposition of discipline, Cawthorn was able to raise the funds needed in order to stock his library. These funds were not recorded in the Skinners' records and could be used by the headmaster independently of any guidance from the Governors. The bibliophile headmaster could use the funds raised through disciplinary fines to purchase books from his wide range of contacts and associates amongst the London publishing and bookselling community. This in turn reinforced his influence and standing amongst this constituency and helped to encourage further patronage of Tonbridge School by the London literati.

However, it was also the case that in the process of establishing this virtuous circle of dependency, The Rev. James Cawthorn, Headmaster of Tonbridge School (1743-1761), laid the foundations of his subsequent reputation as the disciplinary despot of Tonbridge School headmasters.

CHAPTER SEVEN
Cawthorn's Legacy

Barry Orchard in his book, *A Look at the Head and the Fifty*, when discussing Cawthorn, makes the observation that:

> "His reputation for severity does not seem to fit with his passion for music and poetry" [1].

There is indeed much with the accepted historical narrative that sits uncomfortably with the available historical evidence when trying to assess Cawthorn's legacy.

The success of his library, however, is beyond doubt.

Cawthorn's Library Legacy

James Cawthorn became Headmaster of Tonbridge School in 1743. Prior to Cawthorn's appointment a number of his predecessors, from Christopher Wase to Richard Spencer, had tried with varying degrees of success to firmly establish a school library at Tonbridge. With the greater affordability and availability of books in the eighteenth century, the failure to develop the library was becoming an increasingly serious issue for the school if it wished to establish itself as a destination academic institution capable of competing with the likes of Eton, Westminster and Winchester. Cawthorn was fundamentally different from his predecessors in so far as he possessed both the character and the background to ensure that during his tenure as headmaster, Tonbridge School would get its first recognisable school library building, furnished with a collection of books of which the school could be proud. He used the inheritance he received from the sale of his father's lead mines to underwrite the building of a new study which for a hundred years after his death would be referred to as the Cawthorn Library. Within this building was housed a collection of books which Cawthorn had inherited on his appointment and had subsequently added to throughout his tenure as headmaster. The methods Cawthorn used in order to expand the library's collection were ingenious in their simplicity and reflected the character of their architect. He used his reputation and the esteem with which he was held by the printing and bookselling community to attract pupils to the school and to reinforce his contacts within this constituency. His highly original and targeted use of the school rule book and the manner in which he dispensed discipline within the school ensured a regular source of funds which he could lavish upon the booksellers by buying the latest volumes for his school library. In the centuries after his death, his enduring legacy would be shaped by his resulting reputation for disciplinary severity. However, in the immediate aftermath of his death, his most obvious legacy to Tonbridge School was evident in the remarkable collection of books he left in the newly built Cawthorn Library.

Books Galore!

During a Court of Assistants meeting convened on the 26th May 1761, a month after James Cawthorn's death, two members of the Skinners' Company, Mr Joshua Lewis and Mr John Winterton, were assigned to visit Tonbridge in order,

> "… that an inventory or Schedule be made and taken of such Fixtures, Goods and Effects as shall appear to belong to this Company… and also a Catalogue of the books in the school" [2].

This procedure had been followed before on a change of headmaster, regardless of the circumstances of the change and was a requirement laid down in Sir Andrew Judd's original statutes for the school where "it is willed" that:

> "… The Company of Skinners have an inventory in their hands of all things that appertain unto the School, be they books or implements in the Master's or Usher's house. So that at the parting they may be stayed to the schools behalf" [3].

The school archives contain a copy of the catalogue of books made on the appointment of Cawthorn's predecessor Richard Spencer.

A new catalogue was subsequently produced in 1743 when Cawthorn became headmaster and a copy of this book is also held in the school archives. The decision to produce it was made at a Court of Assistants meeting held on the 27th September 1743 to confirm Cawthorn's appointment as Headmaster of Tonbridge, where it was agreed that the Clerk of the Company, Mr Russell, was to accompany to the school a committee of members whose task was to:

"... see a Catalogue made of the books and an inventory taken of the goods and things in the said school" [4].

The 1743 catalogue made at the time of Cawthorn's appointment highlights the influence of Spencer in the evolution of the library at Tonbridge in so far as, in this catalogue, the books are listed into eight groups ranked from A to H which presumably denotes upon which of Spencer's eight bookshelves they usually resided. There were 636 books listed in the catalogue at the time of Cawthorn's appointment, which suggests that during the school's first 200 or so years, approximately three books were bought on average each year.

A month after Lewis and Winterton were assigned their task, they reported back to the Skinners at a Committee of Leases held on the 24th June 1761. At this meeting a series of payments were authorised to be paid to Cawthorn's sister and sole executor of his will, Elizabeth Cawthorn, to cover a number of items of expenditure at the school incurred by James Cawthorn but not previously authorised, or indeed, reported to the Skinners. These included, for example, the installation of a bath, a boiler to provide hot water and a new oven in the kitchen which:

"… were erected by the late Mr Cawthorne at his own expense" [5].

Items of which the Governors had been completely unaware he had even commissioned. No mention was made of the catalogue of books which had also been requested.

The reason for this early silence surrounding the catalogue soon becomes apparent, however, when at a Court of Assistants meeting held on the 15th July 1761 the two stocktakers were forced to report that despite now having had two months in which to prepare it,

"… the catalogue of the books in the said school not being yet completed the delivery there of was postponed to a further time" [6].

The next Court of Assistants meeting was held on the 15th October 1761 when further payments were authorised to be made to Elizabeth Cawthorn to cover, for example,

"Paper Hangings in several apartments of the said school house together with a Copper Pot and Brass Cover… " [7]

Items which Cawthorn had again commissioned and paid for himself but had once more not felt fit to report to the Governors. The catalogue of books in the library, meanwhile, had still not been completed such that,

> "Mr Joshua Lewis, one of the members of this Court, postponed the delivery of the Catalogue of Books belonging to this Company at the school at Tonbridge taken by him and Mr John Winterton, another member of this Court" [8].

It was now over six months since Cawthorn's death and the Skinners were becoming increasingly exasperated by the inability to complete the catalogue of books in the library; such was the scale of the task. Lewis and Winterton had repeatedly postponed the delivery of the catalogue of books in Cawthorn's library because of their inability to complete what had become an infinitely more significant task than had been the case on, for example, Cawthorn's appointment as headmaster. It was no longer a case of merely documenting six hundred or so volumes, neatly stacked on eight bookshelves at the end of the schoolroom. They were instead faced with literally walls of books, housed in a purpose-built "room for books" which was beyond anything the school had previously owned.

In the end it appears that they gave up and the catalogue was quietly dropped without having ever been completed, for at a Court of Assistants meeting held on the 14th May 1762, over a year after Cawthorn's untimely death, it was,

> "Ordered that the sum of five guineas be paid by Mr Gregg this Company's Receiver to Mr Joshua Lewis and Mr John Winterton for their pains and

trouble in taking an Inventory of the Fixtures, Goods and Effects belonging to this Company at the School House in Tunbridge pursuant to an order of (this) Court" [9].

No mention was made of the catalogue of books which had also been requested. There is indeed no further reference in the Skinners' Court records to the catalogue of books that should have been compiled on Cawthorn's death and the subsequent appointment of Johnson Towers. Likewise, on Towers' death in January 1772, and at the subsequent Court of Assistants meeting which appointed his successor Vicesimus Knox, no mention is made of the requirement to visit Tonbridge and compile a catalogue of the school's collection of books. The Skinners' Company had evidently decided that Cawthorn's library legacy to the school was on such a scale that this was a requirement of the school's original statutes with which it was now no longer practicable to comply. Indeed, so great had been the increase in the number of books during Cawthorn's tenure as headmaster and since his library was built that years later, when Dr Vicesimus Knox was questioned by the Skinners about the need for a new catalogue of books, he replied,

"… the arrangement of the Books according to the catalogue had been many years previously totally changed in consequence of the removal of them from the School Room, where to their great injury they all formerly stood, to the study (ie: Cawthorn's Library). The catalogue therefore… was become obsolete" [10].

It is apparent from the Skinners' Company records that by the time of Cawthorn's death he had bequeathed Tonbridge School a legacy of a library of books on a scale beyond anything the school had previously owned. They were now housed in a separate and purpose-built "room for books", rather than merely stored on shelves at the end of the schoolroom. Cawthorn had succeeded where his predecessors had failed in finally establishing a clearly recognisable school library at Tonbridge, thus enabling the school to begin the journey towards firmly establishing itself amongst the destination academic institutions for the education of boys [11].

Beyond the Library

It is also evident from the available records that Cawthorn bequeathed Tonbridge School much more than just the Cawthorn Library. He also left the school buildings in general and the physical fabric of the institution in a much greater state of repair and a more inviting place than he had found on his arrival. Hot water had been installed and the rooms were decorated with what was at the time the latest fashion of "paper wall hangings" – or wallpaper, as it is more commonly known today. Although the Skinners' Company footed the bill for most of these improvements, it is also the case that Cawthorn quite regularly paid for improvements from his own pocket. It was the same combination of his character and his family background which had resulted in the development of the library that also provided both the impetus and the means to deliver these further improvements.

The sale of the lead mines after his father's death had provided Cawthorn and his siblings with a degree of financial independence which James had used to good effect during the remainder of his own lifetime. There is an indication in James Cawthorn's will [12] of quite how financially comfortable he was at the time of his own death. He left £500 to his surviving brother, Charles – the London merchant and member of the Skinners' Company; his second sister Mary received £250; his mother £100 and his youngest sister, Sarah, £50. The bulk of his estate, however, including his own collection of books, was left to the sister he appears to have been closest to, his elder sister Elizabeth. This balance of his estate, as well as providing for Elizabeth, was also to provide an annuity income for life for his mother of £30 per annum and his youngest sister, Sarah, who was still living at home, of £15 per annum. An indication of how much Elizabeth received can be appreciated by reference to the subsequent will of her only child, Edward Goodwin junior [13], who on his own death left over £2000 despite having apparently given away the bulk of his mother's fortune during the course of his own life.

Beyond the Books

But Cawthorn's legacy is not just about the physical improvements he made at Tonbridge during his tenure as headmaster, but is also about the boys he taught.

The story behind the first library built at Tonbridge

School forms the central narrative of Cawthorn's legacy to the school and is the key to understanding the man himself. However, his legacy extended beyond mere bricks and mortar and indeed beyond the undoubtedly substantial library of books he left the school, but also lived on in the impression he made on the lives of his pupils. In this regard, the historical evidence again suggests a somewhat different legacy than that portrayed in the histories of the school. Cawthorn's impact on the lives of the boys he taught ran deep, as is evidenced by the compulsion experienced by one of his more prominent pupils after the death of his headmaster.

After James Cawthorn's death, Sir Sampson Gideon, who whilst still a pupil at Tonbridge had been created a baronet in 1759, received a letter from an old school friend. It was dated from Chiddingstone, May 26th 1761, lamenting their late headmaster's death and eulogising his memory. Despite his challenging experiences under Cawthorn's tutelage, Gideon still felt compelled to send the verses to the *Gentleman's Magazine* where they were reprinted and addressed to "The Memory of the Rev. Mr Cawthorn, late Master of Tunbridge School". They give an inspiring insight into the feelings of ex-pupils towards their old master:

"Come, ever-musing melancholy, come
Pow'rless of utt'rance, come, heart-bursting grief,
Bring all your sad solemnities of woe,
And in the mournful measure of the grave,
Support my wounded strength to Medway's vale.
There weakness will be praise: the tear that flows

From holy Friendship's eye is register'd
For future joys, when tears can flow no more.
Cold, cold and lifeless is the hand that wove
Th' unfading wreath of plenty and of peace
To crown the brows and bless the heart of want;
Breathless the breast that never breath'd a wish
But piety to God, or good to man;
And mute, for ever mute, the hallow'd lip
That made e'en Envy Virtue. O thou stream,
Be witness for me when he touch'd the reed,
How have the wandering herds forgot to graze,
How have those thousand various hues that deck
Thy lovely banks, and sip thy silver dew,
Flush'd their gay bloom, and pour'd forth all their sweets.
Thou too be witness, for he cheer'd thy shades,
High favour'd grove, and charm'd thy dusky gloom
With sounds that angels might have stoop'd to hear.
Yes, Gideon, yes, the blast, bleak blast that froze
Our Cawthorn's spring, nipt too thy opening bud.
He lov'd thee much sweet youth! For thee explor'd
The classic page, and thro' the living line
Pointed each bright example as it rose:
From Tarquin's lustful brow tore Glory's crown,
And rais'd triumphant Virtue from the plough:
Taught thee the mighty Caesar on his throne,
Amidst his millions of applauding slaves,
Beam'd less, illustrious monarch of the globe,
Than Brutus bleeding on Pharsalia's plain.
He read the skies, and in the vast expanse

> Where worlds unnumber'd float, and worlds are lost,
> Led thee thro' Nature up to Nature's God.
> Yet more – he lifted thine adoring eye
> To scenes beyond the skies, and fir'd the soul
> With longings after bliss, immortal bliss,
> When earth shall melt, and stars and suns be dust,
> O may mine ear, midst all the pride of wealth,
> And all the luxuries and pomps of state,
> 'Midst all the passions health and youth inspire,
> And all the charms a sprightly fancy paints,
> O may thine ear indelibly retain
> That truth eternal of the saint we mourn:
> "He must be good who wishes to be great."'[14]

The poem illustrates that his pupils had learnt the fundamental lesson of life underpinning Cawthorn's teaching – it didn't matter whether or not a person held a title or what place they occupied in the world; what mattered was who they were as an individual and what type of person they aspired to be. Just as the young George Austen had preached to the Skinners' Company delegation on the visitation in 1746; virtue was what mattered. In order to be great, one first had to be good.

Cawthorn and the Austens

Elizabeth Cawthorn was the sole executor of her brother's will, but of course, given the pattern of James Cawthorn's life, it is inevitable that an Austen features in his Last

Will and Testament. This time, however, it is not George Austen's name that appears but is instead Thomas Austen, another of George's uncles, who after being educated at Sevenoaks had moved back to Tonbridge where he became an apothecary. Thomas appears as a witness to Cawthorn's will and as such the two men must have known each other well. He was obviously somebody Cawthorn trusted and whose friendship he valued. Thomas' son Henry Austen had been Head Boy at Tonbridge when George Austen first entered the school and had matriculated at Queens' College, Cambridge for the Michaelmas term of 1743, the year Cawthorn became headmaster. At the time of Henry's matriculation one of the Fellows of Queens', Morley Unwin, was engaged to be married to Mary Cawthorne, daughter of William Cawthorne, a draper from Ely, distant cousins of the Cawthorns of Sheffield and possibly the family with whom Cawthorn lodged during his brief time as a student at Cambridge University. Mary Unwin (nee Cawthorne) would later, after the death of her husband, become famous for her care and devotion to the poet William Cowper, whose poetry would in turn be much appreciated by George Austen. In 1759 Henry, who had taken holy orders, had been granted the curacy of Steventon in Hampshire which had been in the gift of a distant relative, Thomas Knight.

It is surprising in many respects that George Austen is not mentioned in James Cawthorn's will. After all, the two men had known each other for two decades and had probably first met when George was a young, recently orphaned boy living in his Uncle Stephen's bookshop. Cawthorn had been Austen's tutor throughout most of his education at Tonbridge, during which time he had taken every opportunity to promote the interests of his young pupil with the Skinners' Company which in turn had helped George to gain a fellowship to St John's, Oxford, reserved for boys from Tonbridge School. On completion of his studies he had returned to Tonbridge where Cawthorn had employed him as his deputy, or Usher, a post which included accommodation and therefore meant the young orphan not only had a job, but also a house in which to live when not at college.

Austen's time as Usher to Cawthorn at Tonbridge is both confusing and revealing. Brian Southam highlights in *George Austen: Pupil, Usher and Proctor* that:

> "There has always been confusion about George Austen's exact years as Usher. Some histories of the School say 1754 to 1758, others 1758 to 1761"[15].

The source of the uncertainty is the Skinners' Court records which are indeed unclear on this point and again it is the Cawthorn Library which appears to be the central cause of the confusion. George Austen's name appears on a number of occasions in the Skinners' Court records and when considered in conjunction with other historical sources, it is possible to establish a picture of George's academic career which helps to explain both the confusion about his time as Usher at Tonbridge and also his relationship with James Cawthorn.

James Cawthorn's legacy to George Austen is typical of the enigmatic character who bequeathed so much to Tonbridge School. The Cawthorn Library once again forms the central narrative of the story.

CHAPTER EIGHT
Austen's Legacy

The story behind the first library built at Tonbridge School is, of course, about more than just Cawthorn's legacy to the school. It also represents the central narrative of the story about the relationship between James Cawthorn and George Austen. The successful development of the library was central to their partnership at Tonbridge and the achievements of Cawthorn owed much to the support of his deputy. Cawthorn's legacy is also Austen's legacy. For George Austen, however, his legacy from Tonbridge School is as important as his contribution to the school. The saga surrounding the formation of Cawthorn's Library results in a uniquely ambiguous legacy to George Austen from Tonbridge School's most enigmatic headmaster.

Educating George Austen

George Austen first appears in Hart's School Register for Tonbridge when he is shown as having joined the school for the academic year 1740/41[1]. The list for May 1741 lists George as 42nd in the school with an 'N' next to his name denoting that he was new to the school and probably joined for the Michaelmas term, 1740, after having moved back to Tonbridge to stay with his aunt, Elizabeth Hooper. He would have been nine years old. Cawthorn became headmaster in September of 1743 and chose George to be one of the scholars to be tested by the Skinners' appointed examiner in May 1744[2], the first visitation to Tonbridge during Cawthorn's tenure. By this time, despite still only being a youngster, he was nevertheless ranked 5th in the school, in an admittedly much depleted year group and his academic abilities were clearly recognised by his headmaster who was keen to ensure that the visiting Skinners would also be impressed. As he turned fifteen, he was once again impressing the visiting Skinners' delegation as he recited Cawthorn's *Equality of Human Conditions* in May 1746 after which he was rewarded with a Fellowship at St John's College, Oxford, reserved for a Tonbridge School boy.

George matriculated on 2nd July 1747 [3]. The St John's College archives contain the Fellows' accounts or "battels" which give an indication of how much each Fellow spent on board and lodgings during an academic year. This gives an indication of a Fellow's attendance during term time which can be cross referenced against the "Register of Absences" records also held by St John's. The pattern of expenses for George is as one would expect in the case of an undergraduate. He had relatively high expenses compared to his academic peers at St John's during the academic year 1747/8 as he settled into college. These expenses are to a modest extent offset by the small stipend he received through his Sir Thomas White Tonbridge Fellowship [4]. He would, however, most likely have still needed some additional external financial support and this may well have continued to come from his Uncle Francis, who had paid his school fees whilst he was a pupil at Tonbridge. For the following three years of his studies, George's battels averaged approximately £5 per term in each of the four terms of the academic years until he graduated as a Bachelor of Arts in 1751[5]. During his final year he also received the benefit of a college exhibition[6] and on graduation his stipend increased significantly, albeit to a still fairly modest level[7]. Throughout his time as an undergraduate, George appeared to be a particularly diligent student and took very few "leaves of absences". However, on graduation he did allow himself a modest break from college before returning to study for his MA[8].

George Austen was awarded his MA in 1754 and once again throughout his course of study he appeared, by reference to his battels, to have been a diligent student. Although his expenses were lower than during his undergraduate days, reflecting a less pressing need to be in college, they were, nevertheless, higher than the average for the other postgraduate students at St John's. His "leave of absences" were once again very low with the exception of a period at the end of his studies. His income also increased, not only as a result of his higher Fellowship stipend but also as a result of him being awarded a number of college exhibitions in both 1753[9] and 1754[10], which on average provided him with an extra £5 per term.

Further support from the Skinners' Company

The Skinners' Company records also record that at a Court of Assistants meeting held on the 19th October, 1753,

"... the Petition of Mr George Austen, an orphan now a student at St John's College in Oxford (who was educated at Tunbridge School) was read for an Exhibition of Sir Thomas Smiths Gift... " [11]

After due consideration it was decided that,

"... the same was conferred on the said George Austen. To hold according to the Will of the said Sir Thomas Smith and the Good Pleasure of this Company, some good person executing a bond as usual" [12].

Prior to receiving the Smith's Exhibition, George is recorded in the Register of Absences at St John's as having taken an extended leave of absence from the 3rd July 1753 until the 15th November of the same year, which covers the period during which his petition was heard [13].

By the summer of 1753 George Austen was a young man in his early 20s who it appears was having to increasingly make his own financial way in the world. Family financial support from the likes of his Uncle Francis may have been somewhat less forthcoming as George reached early adulthood and he was increasingly dependent upon his own talents in order to fund his continuing education. In this regard, his outstanding academic abilities and his diligent work ethic enabled him to win support in the form of exhibitions from both his Oxford college and the benefactors of his old school, the Worshipful Company of Skinners. In the case of the latter, he was undoubtedly helped by the way in which his headmaster, James Cawthorn, had consistently promoted his interests whilst he was at Tonbridge. Listed in the attendance column amongst the small number of members in attendance for the October 1753[14] Court of Assistants meeting at which Austen was awarded a Smith's Exhibition, is Mr Henry Buckle who had been one of the Skinners who had made the journey to Tonbridge for the 1744 visitation when George Austen had been one of the pupils facing the examiner [15]. Also listed is Mr Timothy Mathews who was another Skinner who had been a member of the 1744[16] delegation and who had also been present at the 1746[17] visitation to hear George Austen reciting Cawthorn's poetry on equality. Given that George appears in the Register of Absences as having been away from college in October 1753, he probably presented his petition in person and would have been known and most likely recognised by at least some of the committee members. The Skinners' accounts ledger shows that the first payment to Austen on his Smith's Exhibition was paid in arrears in June 1754, covering the preceding "three quarters of a year" [18]. In other words it covered the period from the beginning of the Michaelmas term in September of 1753. From 1754, however, James Cawthorn's financial support for his ex-pupil extended beyond the assistance he had provided in helping George to win both his White's Scholarship and his Smith's Exhibition.

Further support from James Cawthorn

The year 1754 was a seminal year for James Cawthorn. It was the year in which he lost both his younger brother Thomas Cawthorn and his father, Thomas Senior. It was also the year in which his old friend and colleague Johnson Towers resigned his position as Usher at Tonbridge School. Johnson Towers had been Cawthorn's deputy since January 1746 when he had taken over from the then incumbent, Rowland Atkinson. The school's founder, Sir Andrew Judd, made clear in the school statutes that the appointment of Usher was exclusively in the gift of the headmaster – "… the Master always appoint and elect the Usher as often as the place shall be void, whom so appointed and presented to the said Company of Skinners, I desire them to admit him…" [19]. This obviously makes sense, as it clearly has to be a person whom the headmaster feels he is capable of working alongside in the classroom. The annual salary paid to the Usher, which is also stipulated in the school statutes, is in effect, therefore, a stipend which is in the gift of the headmaster to award to whomsoever he chooses. This salary was usually paid in arrears at the end of the school year. The payments to Johnson Towers in June 1755 and George Austen in June of 1756, recorded in the Skinners' payments ledger, suggest that the two men overlapped with each other during the Michaelmas term beginning in September 1754, before George took over sole responsibility for the role of Usher from January 1755 [20].

From the date of George assuming the position of Usher during the Michaelmas term of 1754, the Skinners' payments ledger records him as being paid the salary as prescribed in the school statutes for every year up to and including 1761, the year of Cawthorn's death. The final payment was made in October 1761 when there was,

"... paid one quarter salary due at Lady day of £1 and 5 shillings" [21].

This payment was made at the same time as a payment was made covering James Cawthorn's salary for the same period as evidenced by the following entry,

"... paid Elizabeth Cawthorne, Extrix of the late Rev. Mr Cawthorne, dec'd one quarter salary due at Lady Day 1761, £2 and 10 shillings" [22].

The payments to Austen are recorded on pages headed "George Austen – Usher" and cover a period of time which extends beyond Austen's tenure as Usher. However, from the point of Cawthorn's death, the heading "George Austen" has a line drawn through it and subsequent Usher's payments are simply recorded as "Payments to Usher of Tunbridge School" [23].

The inference from the Skinners' payments ledgers is clear; when James Cawthorn used the authority vested in him by the school statutes to choose an Usher, he appointed George Austen in 1754, and the appointment was intended to be of a long term nature. It is quite possible and indeed highly likely that Cawthorn intended that in the fullness of time, George Austen would succeed him as Headmaster of Tonbridge School. Such a move would be an obvious and natural transition: Cawthorn had known George since childhood and was fully aware of his talent and understood his character; Cawthorn was also well acquainted with other members of the Austen family; the Austens were a well-known and respected local family and George had been born in Tonbridge. Most importantly however, George also knew and understood James Cawthorn; he had been educated by him; he had witnessed the highs and lows of James' life, including the death of his wife and young daughters; he understood Cawthorn's ambitions for Tonbridge School and most importantly in this respect, Cawthorn's desire to, once and for all, build a library at the school, and the means by which he went about fulfilling this ambition.

George Austen and Cawthorn's Library

The timing of Austen's appointment as Usher in the context of the story of Cawthorn's library is very significant. George Austen assumed sole responsibility for the position of Tonbridge School Usher under James Cawthorn in January 1755. This was the year in which Thomas Cawthorn's estate was settled and James Cawthorn's personal financial situation was transformed. It was also the year in which Cawthorn finalised the plans which he presented in January 1756 to the Skinners' Company for the "... pulling down and new building the Masters Study... "[24], that is, the building of the Cawthorn Library, to be financially underwritten by the headmaster. The year 1756 was the year in which the new library was built and, early the following year the books were transferred from the old schoolroom into the newly built library. It is notable that throughout this period, indeed from March 1754 until July of 1757, George Austen took an extended "leave of absence" from St John's College [25]. He was present at Tonbridge, supporting James Cawthorn throughout the period when the new school library building was planned, built and completed. In this regard, he played a crucial supporting role as Cawthorn's vision was turned into reality. The physical creation of the Cawthorn Library was, in effect, the result of a partnership between James Cawthorn and George Austen. Who better to succeed Cawthorn at some future date in order to safeguard and develop the Cawthorn Library legacy, than George Austen?

Unfortunately, Austen's tenure as Usher also witnessed the debacle of the failure to complete the sale of the Sandhills Estate to the Foundling Hospital. This episode, taken together with the necessity of Tonbridge's headmaster to financially underwrite the development of the school's estate, served to highlight the less than satisfactory state of the Skinners' Company's finances. The subsequent actions taken by the Skinners to get their financial house in order had unfortunate consequences for Austen and helped to create the confusion surrounding his tenure as Usher.

Repercussions of the Sandhills Debacle

At a Court of Assistants meeting held on the 10th December 1756 [26] it was clear that the Skinners' Company intended to get its financial affairs in order. First of all an investigation was ordered into the arrears outstanding on the rents due from tenants in the Skinners' property estate. Attention then turned to the expenditure side of the Skinners' accounts ledgers and inquiries were ordered into the payments made for exhibitions awarded by the Company.

The financial inquisition did not, however, stop with the investigations into rent arrears and the awarding of exhibitions. Tonbridge School also found itself under scrutiny and, in particular, the expenditure incurred by the headmaster on the day-to-day running of the school. In this regard, it appears from an interpretation of the available historical evidence that James Cawthorn came under pressure to explain and justify his decision to employ George Austen as his Usher.

George Austen had been awarded a Skinners' Company exhibition from September 1753 in order for him to continue his studies at Oxford University. It was most likely assumed therefore by the Skinners that he would spend his time studying in Oxford. However, the following year James Cawthorn used the power vested in him by the Tonbridge School statutes to employ Austen as his deputy on an annual salary paid for by the Skinners' Company. The Usher's salary was also supplemented each year by an annual gratuity which was paid at the discretion of the Skinners and ensured that the resulting level of overall remuneration was comparable to teaching posts of a similar level at other schools. In practice this gratuity was voted through at a Court of Assistants meeting and the name of the Usher receiving the payment was recorded in the court records.

When Austen took over from Towers, the two Ushers overlapped for a term and the subsequent entry in the court books alludes to this point when,

> "Ordered that 10 guineas be given to Mr Cawthorne to be given to the late or present Usher of the said school or to be divided between them as he shall think of it, as a gratuity for their good behaviour as Usher" [27].

From 1754 George Austen found himself in an unusual, albeit a highly remunerative, position. On the one hand, he held the position of White's scholar at St John's, Oxford which was reserved for a boy educated at Tonbridge School and he received a modest stipend as a result. He was also in receipt of a Sir Thomas Smith's scholarship from the Skinners' Company to facilitate his studies at Oxford. On the other hand, he was employed by the Headmaster of Tonbridge School in the role of Usher and as such received a teaching salary paid for by the Skinners' Company. This in turn was supplemented by an annual gratuity voted on and, once again, paid for by the Skinners. All of the Skinners' Company payments to Austen are recorded in the Skinners' Payments Ledger and Court records.

It is not clear whether the Skinners were aware of the fact that they would be paying Austen to both study at Oxford whilst also simultaneously paying him to teach at Tonbridge at the time that Cawthorn appointed him as Usher. What is clear, however, is that all of these payments came under scrutiny during the financial inquisition that was undertaken by the Skinners in the wake of the Sandhills debacle.

Results of the Financial Inquisition

The first of the payments to Austen to be questioned was the Sir Thomas Smith Exhibition when the Skinners' Company wrote to various Oxbridge colleges enquiring whether or not the recipients of the scholarships awarded by the Skinners were actually in residence at college. They then followed up with enquiries to Cawthorn as is evidenced by the following entry as recorded in the court records for a Committee of Leases meeting held on the 18th February 1757:

"Ordered that Mr Raynor (Committee Secretary) do write to the Rev. Mr Cawthorne to acquaint him that the Company being apprehensive that the Exhibitions of Sir Thomas Smith's Gift enjoyed by Thomas Dalyson and Mr George Austen are vacant and that they desire to be informed by him whether the said Mr Dalyson and Mr Austen are within the terms of the Will or not" [28].

Cawthorn's response to this enquiry is not recorded but it was clearly deemed inadequate, for at a Committee of Leases meeting held on the 25th March 1757, the following is noted:

"... It appearing to this committee that Mr George Austen and Mr Thomas Dalyson, two of Sir Thomas Smiths Exhibitioners, do not reside at the University agreeable to the intention of the Donor's Will..." [29]

It was therefore,

"... Resolved that it is the opinion of this committee that the said two last exhibitions be also declared vacant" [30].

This decision was ratified at a Court of Assistants meeting held on the same day such that,

"... exhibitions of Sir Thomas Smith in the room of Mr Thomas Dalyson and Mr George Austen were declared void..." [31]

Presumably, in order to avoid any future misunderstandings it was also,

"Ordered that the Clause in Sir Thomas Smith's Will relating to the Exhibitions thereby given for the benefit of poor scholars educated in Tunbridge School be copyed and sent to Mr Cawthorne..." [32]

Whilst at the same time it was further ordered that,

"... notice be given to Messrs Alexander, Hingston, Dalyson and Austen that the exhibitions formerly conferred on them are declared vacant" [33].

Austen was clearly not the only Oxbridge scholar to fall foul of the major campaign instigated by the Skinners at the end of 1756 to get their financial house in order. The failure to sell the Sandhills Estate, perhaps combined with a degree of uneasiness or embarrassment felt by some members of the Skinners' Company at witnessing their headmaster underwriting the development of their school library in Tonbridge, nevertheless resulted in a response that had unfortunate consequences for George Austen. Ironically, it was shortly after he had lost his Smith's exhibition that Austen returned to Oxford in July of 1757 in order to continue his studies. Despite now being dependent upon his Usher's position for a significant part of his annual income he was nevertheless able to leave Tonbridge and return to Oxford. This decision must have been sanctioned by Cawthorn and according to the Skinners' Payments Ledgers, Cawthorn continued to pay Austen the salary due to the Usher despite him no longer residing in Tonbridge. This appears to have been a direct challenge to the authority of the Skinners' Company and it did not, in turn, go unanswered.

The confusion surrounding Austen's tenure as Usher

With the new study building completed and the school's collection of books expanding rapidly, it was apparent that by the summer of 1757 James Cawthorn and George Austen had succeeded in finally and firmly establishing a library at Tonbridge School. The establishment of the Cawthorn Library had, however, not been without controversy and ultimately cost George Austen his Smith's Exhibition. Perhaps it was as a result of the controversy surrounding the library that George decided to return to Oxford, or maybe he was merely keen to continue with his studies. It was equally true that St John's was also now home to a young undergraduate called James Leigh who had a rather engaging younger sister called Cassandra whose acquaintance George may well have wished to pursue. Whatever the reason George left Tonbridge and returned to Oxford, he did so with James Cawthorn's blessing. This is clear from the fact that Cawthorn continued to pay George the salary due to the Usher of Tonbridge School and, at least initially, he was also paid the annual Usher's gratuity. The Skinners may well have declared as void Austen's exhibition, but Cawthorn, through his actions, makes clear that he was not about to abandon the young man whose academic career he had taken every opportunity to further and whose assistance had been invaluable in helping Cawthorn realise his vision for Tonbridge School. The lives of the two men had by now been interwoven for nearly two decades, and by the summer of 1757 this did not appear to be about to change.

According to the Skinners' payments ledgers it appears that Cawthorn used the power vested in him as Headmaster of Tonbridge to ensure that Austen continued to receive the salary due to the Usher right up until the occasion of Cawthorn's death in April 1761. The same, however, cannot be said of the annual gratuity usually paid to the Usher which was ultimately at the discretion of the Skinners' Company. Initially, this was also paid to Austen but in May of 1758 the following entry appears in the Skinners' Court records in relation to the Usher's gratuity:

> "Ordered that 10 guineas be paid to the late and present Ushers of the said school in such proportion as the Master of the Company and Mr Cawthorne shall think of it" [34].

This was the first time that the Skinners had not left the payment of the gratuity to the discretion of the headmaster but had instead chosen to intervene and assert their authority over the disbursement. It may of course be the case that Cawthorn had always intended that, whereas Austen would continue to be paid the Usher's salary, the gratuity would be used to pay the costs of providing some additional teaching support for Cawthorn to cover for Austen's absence. On his return to Oxford, Austen had taken on some paid appointments at the university and therefore had some income in addition to that which Cawthorn provided him with by way of salary payments. The gratuity therefore offered Cawthorn a degree of financial flexibility and the involvement of the Skinners could arguably be viewed as a means of adding legitimacy to the division of the gratuity decided upon by Cawthorn. What is more likely, however, is that the Skinners were unhappy with Cawthorn's decision to continue paying Austen an Usher's salary after he had returned to Oxford, given that they had withdrawn his exhibition because they felt he no longer deserved to receive it. Whatever the circumstances behind this unusual arrangement, it continued up until Cawthorn's death and is the source of the confusion surrounding Austen's tenure as Usher at Tonbridge School.

The situation was only finally brought to an end after Cawthorn's untimely death in 1761 when the following series of entries is recorded in the Skinners' records. In the minutes to the Court of Assistants meeting held on 21st May 1761 it was,

> "Ordered that 30 guineas be paid to Miss Cawthorne, sole executor of the Rev. Mr James Cawthorne late Master of Tunbridge School deceased, as a Gratuity for the good behaviour of the said Mr Cawthorne as Master of the said school from the Election Day last to the time of his Death" [35].

However, at the same meeting it was also,

> "… Ordered that the Gratuity usually given to the Usher of the said school at Tunbridge be postponed for the consideration of the next Court" [36].

The Skinner's' Company Ledger of Payments, clearly shows that the Usher's salary is paid to George Austen from the date at which he takes over from Johnson Towers in 1754 right up until the death of James Cawthorn in April of 1761.

However, at the Court of Assistants meeting held on the 26th May 1761 at which the payment of the Usher's gratuity is considered, the following entry appears:

> "Ordered that the sum of Ten Guineas be given to the Rev Mr Myles Cooper the late Usher of the said school for his good behaviour during his continuance there in that capacity" [37].

George Austen only unambiguously ceased to be Usher at Tonbridge after the death of his master and mentor in 1761. From the date of his appointment until the date of Cawthorn's death, he was paid the salary due to the Usher and to all intents and purposes, he occupied the position of the Tonbridge School Usher as defined by the school statues; that is, the Usher appointed by the headmaster to act as his deputy. He was also paid the gratuity due to the Usher when he was in residence at Tonbridge. This gratuity was, however, paid to other teachers, who in effect, covered for Austen during his absences from Tonbridge when he was in residence at St John's. Such is the source of the confusion surrounding Austen's tenure as Usher of Tonbridge School.

Cawthorn's legacy to George Austen

James Cawthorn and George Austen most likely met for the first time when George was living in his Uncle Stephen's bookshop and Cawthorn was working as a teacher at the Soho Academy. They met again when Cawthorn moved to Tonbridge with his young wife, Mary, in order to take over as headmaster at George's school. By this time, George had been at Tonbridge School for two years and had been taught by the Rev. Richard Spencer. The quality of the early education he received is open to question as towards the end of Spencer's tenure parents had started to complain about his teaching and the Skinners' Company were also unsure about the wisdom of Spencer remaining in post. For the next four years Austen was taught by Cawthorn, and Brian Southam provides a flavour of the educational legacy that Cawthorn would have provided Austen with:

> "... The 'Grammar' in the School's name carried a special meaning. It meant that the education provided...was devoted to the study of classics, almost entirely Latin literature, with a very small element of Greek... The bottom form started with Aesop and thereafter the progression was from Aesop to Terence, from Terence to Virgil, from Virgil to Cicero and onwards to Caesar, Horace and other Latin authors, ancient and modern. [38]

Additional instruction was also provided by visiting instructors in Writing, Mathematics, French and Dancing.

Cawthorn's style of teaching is also described by Southam in so far as,

> "... All the histories of the School repeat this story: how Cawthorn would throw down on the floor a volume of Virgil or Shakespeare as a prize and challenge 'his pupils to speak a speech against him'" [39].

This in its day was an effective form of teaching, for as Southam goes on to explain,

> "... these contests provided a good preparation for university, since they were along the lines of the formal disputations at Oxford and Cambridge, exercises which formed a major part of the system of examination" [40].

This therefore was the basis of the formal education which Austen received under Cawthorn's tuition. But of course, given Cawthorn's admiration for works by authors such as Fielding and Haywood; his love of the poetry of Pope; his connections to playwrights such as Dodsley and his links to Handel whose music he praises in his poems, it is most likely the case that Austen was encouraged to broaden his reading beyond the confines offered by the school curriculum. Cawthorn may have felt uncomfortable to have his name linked in public to praise for the "base novels" of Henry Fielding, but that does not mean that he did not, in private, encourage his pupil and protégé to read such works.

Cawthorn also took every opportunity to promote the interests of Austen with the Skinners' Company which in turn helped George to win a place at St John's, Oxford and to secure financial support to further his studies. He then employed him in the role of Usher which provided not only a source of income but also a house in his home town of Tonbridge and the prospect of a future career devoted to teaching at his old school.

Austen in turn repaid the support he had received from Cawthorn by taking an extended leave of absence from his studies and providing practical and no doubt moral support to Cawthorn during the period in which the plans for the first school library building at Tonbridge moved quite literally from the drawing board, to become a reality. The gestation of the Cawthorn Library was not, however, without controversy and although Austen returned to Oxford once the library had been firmly established, it was not before he had been stripped of his generous Smith's Exhibition. Cawthorn nevertheless continued to financially support Austen by continuing to pay him the salary due to the Usher and the St John's College archives record "leave of absences" which suggest that George remained a regular visitor to Tonbridge after his return to Oxford. Austen had also taken on the curacy of Shipbourne during his time at Tonbridge [41], and it appears that he clearly harboured ambitions to follow in Cawthorn's steps by combining a full-time teaching position at Tonbridge with some local clergy appointments. Cawthorn, for example, had been curate in the nearby village of Leigh since 1748 in addition to his role as headmaster of Tonbridge [42].

The Unkind Hand of Fate

Unfortunately, Cawthorn's untimely death from a riding accident in April 1761 changed everything. Any hopes the two men may have held about Austen, in the fullness of time, taking over from Cawthorn as Headmaster of Tonbridge School were dashed. Quite apart from the controversy surrounding the building of the Cawthorn Library and Cawthorn's subsequent insistence on continuing to pay Austen an Usher's salary despite him being away at Oxford, it was simply too soon for the Skinners to seriously consider Austen for the role. The Skinners, through force of circumstance in 1743, had been compelled to take a gamble on the appointment of the young and inexperienced Cawthorn, and although in many respects it had turned out to be an inspired choice, Cawthorn's tenure as headmaster had not been without its controversies. They were simply not ready to take the risk of appointing another young and relatively inexperienced master to succeed him. Although Austen would have offered the benefit of continuity, so too did his predecessor as Usher, Johnson Towers, and this was the man the Skinners appointed instead.

Whether coincidental or not, the year of Cawthorn's death, 1761, witnessed a marked increase in the number of short "leaves of absences" recorded for Austen in the St John's College Register of Absences. The impression given is of a young man grappling to come to terms with a dramatic, unexpected and unwelcome change in his circumstances. Cawthorn and Austen may well have both believed that Cawthorn's legacy to Austen would ultimately involve the transfer of the role of Headmaster of Tonbridge School to George whose future life would then evolve as a teaching career supplemented by a number of local clergy positions, similar to the way in which Cawthorn's life had developed. Instead, by the summer of 1761 it was clear that there would be no future for George Austen at Tonbridge School and he would lose his Usher's income. There was in turn no compensating financial legacy from Cawthorn's estate. Cawthorn's will does, however, give a clue as to how Austen's predicament was resolved, for one of the witnesses to the will was, of course, Thomas Austen.

Austen supports Austen

Thomas Austen had lived in Tonbridge virtually all his life and had got to know James Cawthorn very well after the latter became Headmaster of Tonbridge School. Thomas' only son, Henry Austen, had been educated under Richard Spencer and had been Head Boy when his cousin George had started at the school. Thomas would have witnessed George's progress through the school under Cawthorn, his admission into Oxford and his return to Tonbridge to become Cawthorn's deputy. He would have seen the Cawthorn Library taking shape during George's extended leave of absence from his Oxford studies and, given Thomas' obvious friendship with Cawthorn, would have understood, perhaps as much as George, how much the library meant to the headmaster. Cawthorn may well have confided in Thomas about his hopes and ambitions for the future and given that Thomas was George Austen's uncle, the two older men may well have discussed the young man's prospects. Thomas Austen would therefore have been fully aware of the predicament in which George now found himself, and given his understanding of the relationship between the young Austen and his master and mentor James Cawthorn, he quite possibly felt an obligation to both men to try and help the situation. In this regard, he appears to have turned to his son Henry for assistance. It is notable that shortly after George Austen received his final payment of salary from the Skinners in October of 1761[43], Henry Austen resigned his living as Rector of Steventon in November of the same year. He did so in favour of George who was appointed Rector with effect from the 11th November 1761[44].

A Uniquely Ambiguous Legacy

The lives of James Cawthorn and George Austen were interwoven for over twenty years. James Cawthorn had been a near constant presence in the life of the young George Austen throughout his formative years and had taken every opportunity to promote the interests of his young protégé. His legacy to George ran deep and may well have included the expectation that Austen would, in the fullness of time, succeed Cawthorn as Headmaster of Tonbridge School. Unfortunately however, James Cawthorn's untimely death changed everything.

After Cawthorn's death it became clear that George Austen's future would not evolve as a school teacher in Tonbridge whose income was supplemented by some modest clergy positions. Instead, it would evolve as a clergyman in Steventon whose income was supplemented with some modest teaching appointments.

So it was that George Austen, rather than being appointed to nurture the legacy bequeathed to Tonbridge School in the form of Cawthorn's library, instead became in many respects a victim of the saga surrounding the library's foundation.

CHAPTER NINE

Enduring Legacies

James Cawthorn and George Austen may well have hoped that in the fullness of time, Austen would replace Cawthorn as Headmaster of Tonbridge School and the legacy the two men had bequeathed to the school in the form of the Cawthorn Library would be protected and nurtured. Unfortunately, Cawthorn's untimely death, and the saga surrounding the formation of the library meant that this was not to be.

A Legacy without George Austen

After James Cawthorn's death the responsibility for nurturing his legacy to Tonbridge School fell to George Austen's predecessor as Usher, Johnson Towers. Any disagreement there may have been with the Skinners at the time of Towers' departure in 1754 was forgotten and he was confirmed as headmaster at a Court of Assistants meeting held shortly after Cawthorn's death[1]. The continuity that Towers' appointment ensured had the desired effect, for as Hart observes,

> "There was no such exodus of boys on this change of Head Mastership as had marked that caused by the retirement of Mr. Spencer. The great majority of the boys in the School in the last year of Mr. Cawthorn's reign remained on under his successor" [2].

This included the majority of the literary boys, and it is to be presumed that life in the school continued during the decade that marked Towers' tenure in a similar fashion to that which it had been during Cawthorn's time. However, although the school records are not as complete for Towers' tenure as headmaster as they are for Cawthorn's, they do nevertheless show a falling away in numbers on the register during the course of his time in office. Perhaps the best description of Towers' tenure as head is that provided by Barry Orchard:

> "… during his period as Headmaster the school experienced a period of steady, if uneventful, prosperity… " [3]

With Towers, the Governors got the stability offered by continuity and a "safe pair of hands", but it is impossible not to believe that something was lost with the appointment of Towers as Cawthorn's successor. The momentum of improvement and the passion with which Cawthorn approached his role were now absent as Towers appeared content to rest on the laurels of the previous twenty years of achievement. What may have been, if the Governors had shown more ambition, can only be conjecture but it does feel like an opportunity was missed.

To be fair to Towers, the headmaster was not in the most robust of health and he died in January 1772 at the age of only 48. His brief tenure as head had offered stability, but at a price.

However, if momentum had been lost under Towers, it positively collapsed under his successor, Vicesimus Knox. Before his arrival at Tonbridge, Knox was well regarded as "… a distinguished Classical Scholar… " [4]. He had stood against Towers for the appointment as head on Cawthorn's death, but had been overlooked in favour of Cawthorn's previous Usher. On Towers' death, however, Knox was given his opportunity, and the Cawthorn Library appears to have been of particular interest to this learned academic. Unfortunately, the attraction of the library to Knox appears to have been more for his personal use than a valuable legacy which he wished to nurture as a means of promoting the school's reputation and increasing the number of boys seeking to be educated at Tonbridge. Indeed, leaving the school's collection of books in the Cawthorn Library and venturing out of the headmaster's study in order to discharge his duties of educating the boys under his care appears to have been an aspect of his contract of employment that was wholly lost on this studious scholar. So much so, that when he did take the trouble to complete a register of boys at the school, which was an administrative burden that seldom appears to have exercised his time, the few records that do exist show an alarming collapse in numbers. Boys on the register fell to a low of seventeen of whom only eight were boarders. The literati of London whose patronage Cawthorn had so assiduously cultivated, abandoned the school in droves.

George Austen, whose support for Cawthorn had been invaluable during the building of the library, would, after Cawthorn's death in 1761, play no further part in the affairs of Tonbridge School. He returned to reside permanently at St John's College, Oxford where during a term of office as Proctor in 1759-60 he had been "nicknamed 'The Handsome Proctor' on account of his commanding height and outstanding good looks" [5]. He could have chosen to stay at St John's for the rest of his life "if he were prepared to remain celibate" [6], or he could marry and use the clergy position at Steventon, which his cousin Henry had vacated in his favour, to support a wife and family. It can only be left to the imagination what may have been if George Austen had been able to marry and return to the Usher's quarters at Tonbridge School to start a family, who would thus have been raised as the family of a provincial town schoolmaster, instead of the family of a country village clergyman.

Cawthorn's Enduring Legacy as a Disciplinary Despot

Although the fortunes of the school would once again be revived under Knox's son and grandson, who both followed him as headmasters, the original legacy left by Cawthorn was nevertheless squandered by his two immediate successors. The drive, passion and achievement of the Cawthorn years were forgotten as the school slipped into mediocrity and flirted with obscurity. The school was no longer the destination of choice for the literati of London, which it had increasingly become under the bibliophile earlier headmaster. The magnetism that Cawthorn's library had once offered was overlooked and wasted as his legacy was allowed to wither.

The innovative techniques for raising funds for the library, however, pioneered by Cawthorn, do seem to have outlived him. The disciplinary practice of making a donation to either the school monitors or indeed directly to Cawthorn's library most likely continued under his immediate successors and hence generations of Tonbridge schoolboys came to associate the name of Cawthorn with the administration of punishment. It is hardly surprising therefore that schoolboy myths evolved around the memory of the disciplinarian headmaster, and hence, Septimus Rivington's assertion that,

> "… any boy will tell you who Mr Cawthorne was, whilst all the other Head Masters are almost a dead letter to them" [7].

Although initially known as the "Headmaster's Study", the building that Cawthorn commissioned and financially underwrote, soon became recognised as his library and for a hundred years after it was built, the first school library building at Tonbridge was known as the "Cawthorn Library" in recognition of the headmaster who laid its foundations. The triangular association between Cawthorn, the school library and the administration of discipline also became deeply entrenched during this period.

The story behind the first library built at Tonbridge School ensured that the seeds of James Cawthorn's enduring legacy, as the disciplinarian despot of Tonbridge School headmasters, were sown. It is the saga surrounding the foundation of the Cawthorn Library, rather than the curious case of the schoolboy who was killed, that is the source of the myths surrounding Tonbridge School's most controversial and enigmatic headmaster.

CHAPTER TEN

Making Sense of the Enigma

An understanding of James Cawthorn's character and background, and his relationship with George Austen is essential in trying to piece together the story behind the first library built at Tonbridge School. The story of the development of the school library is also central to understanding Cawthorn's tenure as Headmaster of Tonbridge.

It is unfortunate in many respects that successive historians of the school have persisted in perpetuating the same mythological schoolboy nonsense about pupils dying at the hands of an almost demonic tyrant. This preoccupation on a story with no factual historical evidence to support it has been a distraction which has helped to obscure an infinitely more interesting story and has created a narrative which inconveniently fails to fit the available historical evidence.

The Deadweight of History

In trying to make sense of the enigma that is James Cawthorn, in order to better understand his tenure as

Headmaster of Tonbridge, the histories of the school do little in helping to illuminate his character.

Septimus Rivington is the first of the school's historians to portray Cawthorn in largely unflattering terms,

> "... he went to Tonbridge, and gained a reputation for great strictness and severity. His character was peculiar; though harsh in school matters, in society he was pleasant; with a great love of fine arts, he was passionately fond of music, and yet this was almost the only art with which he had no technical acquaintance. He was a bad horseman, but a constant rider" [1].

Rivington has done much to influence subsequent historians of the school and in part this may be because of his position as the great-nephew of one of Cawthorn's pupils, Francis Rivington. Although Francis died before Septimus was born, it is quite possible that stories of his great uncle's schooldays at Tonbridge were passed down through the family and influenced the younger Rivington's writing. If this is the case, his work needs to be treated with some caution. Unlike the majority of the other booksellers and publishers who sent their sons to Tonbridge to be educated by Cawthorn, the Rivingtons in the eighteenth century were primarily publishers of books with a deep theological heritage. This would have instantly placed the young Francis at odds with his more progressive literary classmates, and indeed, with his headmaster whose previous teaching experience had been at one of the leading institutions in the vanguard of the Enlightenment, the Soho Academy. Francis' own demeanour in which "his probity, his piety and his hilarity of disposition"[2] which in later life "endeared him to all who knew him"[3], may also not have been to his advantage in the rough and tumble of the schoolyard at Tonbridge under Cawthorn. It is notable that whereas other literary boys spent some years at Tonbridge during Cawthorn's tenure as headmaster and were often joined by siblings, Francis was only at the school for two years and no other Rivingtons are listed in Hart's school rolls.

Nevertheless, Somervell again takes his lead from Rivington and Cawthorn is thus described as having,

"… left the reputation of a severe disciplinarian, so severe that his ghost remorsefully haunted the school house dormitories for more than a hundred years afterwards" [4]

… and so it came about that the myths surrounding the late headmaster began to evolve.

It is, however, fortunate in some respects that Cawthorn's life has not only been of interest to historians of Tonbridge School. Prior to becoming Headmaster of Tonbridge he was, of course, more widely known as a poet and as such has been of interest to a number of biographers for this aspect of his life.

The Poet's Perspective

Cawthorn appears in Chalmers' *General Biographical Dictionary, Vol.8,* published in 1812[5] and Chalmers also adds an account of Cawthorn's life and poetry in the earlier *The Works of the English Poets from Chaucer to Cowper*, published in 1810[6]. This was a series of volumes on the works of significant English poets originally commissioned from Samuel Johnson prior to his death and subsequently extended by the booksellers and publishers involved in the project.

Chalmers, however, does not appear to have been particularly impressed with Cawthorn's abilities as a poet, for he writes:

> "As a poet, he displays considerable variety of power, yet perhaps he is rather to be placed among the ethical versifiers, than ranked with those who have attempted with success the higher flights of genius. As an imitator of Pope, he is superior to most of those who have formed themselves in that school, yet his imitations are often so close as to appear the effect of memory, than of judgement"[7].

He is rather more flattering when considering Cawthorn's intellectual abilities in so far as:

> "His acquired knowledge must have been very considerable, as his allusions to various branches of the sciences and of political literature are frequent, and bespeak a familiarity with the subject" [8].

However, when it comes to school matters, Chalmers does not stray from the usual familiar territory:

> "We are more in the dark as to his behaviour as a schoolmaster... we are told, that although generous and friendly in the common intercourse of life, he was singularly harsh and severe in the conduct of his school" [9].

Chalmers does, however, suggest that some good may have resulted from Cawthorn's tenure as Headmaster of Tonbridge, for he acknowledges:

> "To the school he was in one respect a useful benefactor. In conjunction with his patrons, he founded the library now annexed to it" [10].

Dr Samuel Johnson had not included Cawthorn in his original series of volumes covering the works of historically important poets first published towards the end of his life. When Cawthorn's work first appeared in the series, in Volume 65 published in 1790, six years after Johnson's death, the first edition promised more than it delivered when on the title page it announces the inclusion of "Prefaces, Biographical and Critical" [11]. The original entry for Cawthorn was, in fact, little more than an almost exact copy of a compilation of Cawthorn's work assembled in 1771 which was published by an ex-pupil, William Woodfall and sold by private subscription [12]. Even the order in which the works are arranged was virtually identical to this earlier work and nothing new was offered in terms of either Cawthorn's poetry or indeed any insights into the character of the man himself. In the preface, apparently attributed to Johnson, it states that:

> "Such as the work now is, I submit it to the public. Defects in it there are many, which I have wanted both time and abilities to amend as I could with. Its merit, if it has any, and I may be allowed to name it, is its being natural and unaffected… "(13)

In fairness, "natural and unaffected" was a self-effacing way of describing a blatant reprint of somebody else's work and the motive for publication is explained later in the preface:

> "Upon the whole, I have sent this my offspring into the world in as decent a dress as I was able; a legitimate one I am sure it is; and if it should be thought defective in strength, spirit, or vigour, let it be considered that its father's marriage with the Muses, like most other marriages into that noble family, was more from necessity than inclination" (14).

The series of books did indeed have undoubted commercial potential and such was Johnson's fame and popularity that by the time of its publication over thirty booksellers and publishers appear on the title page of this volume of the series. Included amongst this list of the great and the good of the publishing world is the firm of John Rivington and Sons, which by this date included Francis Rivington, who having been at Tonbridge under Cawthorn was one of the subscribers to the earlier work published by Woodfall and, of course, may well therefore have provided the copy from which this publication appears to have been taken.

It is a pity that Volume 65 only reproduced the collected folio of Cawthorn's poetry assembled in Woodfall's 1771 publication and did not also add the biographical detail promised on the title page. Johnson's first publisher was, of course, Cawthorn's "worthy friend", Charles Hitch, and his most prolific publishing was done by Robert Dodsley, the same publisher who had sought Cawthorn's opinion on his theatrical production, *The Tragedy of Cleone*. Both Cawthorn and Johnson were patrons of Dolly's Chop House and were involved in the same literary scene in London, albeit in markedly different ways and to a different degree. Johnson would and could, however, have been capable of adding a contemporary account of the man whose work it was felt worthy of inclusion in this series of England's greatest poets and had Cawthorn's work been included earlier, such a contemporary account may well have been forthcoming.

Nevertheless, despite Volume 65's crime of omission it does, in fact, appear to be indirectly responsible for the most detailed and revealing contemporary account of Cawthorn's life. For in 1791, the year after the first publication of Volume 65 of Johnson's *Works of The English Poets*, a detailed account of the life of James Cawthorn appeared in the *Gentleman's Magazine*. It was written by the Rev. Edward Goodwin, who after Cawthorn's death married his sister Elizabeth and would therefore have become his brother-in-law had he still been alive. Elizabeth was the sole executor of Cawthorn's estate and retained possession of his manuscripts and correspondence. These are quoted and referred to extensively in Goodwin's article which is titled *Original*

Memories of Mr James Cawthorn, which is itself a revealing title and may be an allusion to the somewhat less than original work of the previous year.

The Family Connection

Elizabeth Cawthorn's husband, the Rev. Edward Goodwin, provides a comprehensive account of Cawthorn's life and his tenure as Headmaster of Tonbridge School. He explains how a large proportion of Cawthorn's poetry was written for the boys at Tonbridge to recite to the members of the Skinners' Company who travelled down to the school for the annual visitations. He also provides a list of the names of the boys who recited the poems each year. These recitations obviously provided the boys involved with an opportunity to impress the visiting dignitaries, and so it was such that in Goodwin's words:

> "Thus this good man made his poetical abilities subservient to the interests of his pupils"[15].

The most obvious beneficiary in this regard is, of course, George Austen whose interests Cawthorn took every opportunity to promote whilst he was a pupil at the school.

Goodwin goes on to give a thoughtful account of Cawthorn's character, for as he explains,

> "… his literary talents, though very considerable, bore only a small proportion of his moral excellence" [16].

He writes a considerably more nuanced account of Cawthorn's character than the rather one-dimensional view adopted by historians of Tonbridge School and, as such, is worth quoting at length:

> "In the character of a son, he always showed a most respectful and affectionate attention to his parents; as a brother, pursued every proper method to promote the interests of his relations; as a husband, was tender, polite and obliging; as a master, humane, and solicitous for the welfare of his servants. In his school, he supported his station with a becoming dignity; paid a strict regard to his duty; and, without partiality, was ever ready to applaud merit, and discourage indolence. He was hospitable and generous, yet an economist; regular in his accounts, and punctual in the discharge of every just demand; showed a becoming social cheerfulness in company, yet was temperate; and in private, was best pleased with the plainest diet. In a word, those who best knew him had the most reason to value him, and lament his dissolution." [17]

There is much in the above which is recognisable when reviewing the available historical records of Cawthorn's life and his tenure as Headmaster of Tonbridge School; from the close and affectionate relationship he had with his parents and sisters; the help he appears to have extended to his brothers as they established themselves as tradesman in London; his conduct as Headmaster of

Tonbridge and the enduring friendships he made with the likes of Charles Hitch and George Austen.

When viewing Cawthorn's life in the context of the account given by Goodwin, and in light of the evidence in historical records, the schoolboy myth of a child found starved to death in an attic is seen as being not only historically inaccurate but also completely out of character. On the other hand, if the central narrative of the schoolboy who was killed by Cawthorn is dismissed as the mythological nonsense that it undoubtedly is, and the story of the development of the school library at Tonbridge is substituted in its place, the enigma that is James Cawthorn starts to make sense.

Making Sense of the Enigma

James Cawthorn's personal life was not without its moments of tragedy. In particular the death of his wife in 1747, a year after the death of twin daughters who died when only a few days old. The death of the baby girls gave rise to Cawthorn's most celebrated and poignant poem:

A Father's Extempore Consolation on the Death of Two Daughters, who Lived Only Two Days

"Let vulgar souls endure the body's chain
Till life's dull current ebbs in every vein
Dream out a tedious age ere, wide displayed
Death's blackest pinion wraps them in the shade

> These happy infants, early taught to shun
> All that the world admires beneath the sun
> Scorned the weak bands mortality could tie
> And fled impatient to their native sky
>
> Dear precious babes! Alas! When, fondly wild
> A mother's heart hung melting o'er her child
> When my charmed eye a flood of joy expressed
> And all the father kindled in my breast
> A sudden paleness seized each guiltless face
> And death, though smiling, crept o'er every grace
>
> Nature! Be calm – heave not thy impassioned sigh
> Nor teach one tear to tremble in my eye
> A few unspotted moments passed between
> Their dawn of being, and their closing scene:
> And sure no nobler blessing can be given
> When one short anguish is the price of heaven" [18]

Barry Orchard, in *A Look at the Head and the Fifty*, links this episode in Cawthorn's life to his subsequent reputation as a strict disciplinarian:

> "Perhaps his bereavements caused him to be severe, for he had a formidable reputation for severity" [19].

On the contrary, perhaps these bereavements were what drove him with such formidable zeal to take an almost obsessive approach to his library. After all, it was only a few years earlier that his wife's father had made his donation of *Philosophical Transactions* to the embryonic Tonbridge School library. Perhaps the library was to be Cawthorn's memorial to the family he was never to have. His disciplinary severity was merely a means to an end.

Similarly, Cawthorn's treatment of the booksellers is instructive when trying to understand the man behind the myths. He was clearly well regarded by those who sent their boys to Tonbridge to be educated by the apparently severe Master. In this regard, however, it was no disadvantage that, as Goodwin notes, his reputation for "discouraging indolence" was also matched by his willingness to "applaud merit". This can best be illustrated by his treatment of William Woodfall, son of the bookseller Henry Woodfall, who whilst at Tonbridge developed his reputation for the incredible capacity of his memory. The story as told by Rivington and repeated by successive historians of the school is that:

> "His master, Mr Cawthorn, set him one evening a book of Homer to learn by heart, an imposition characteristic of the times in general, and of the master who set it in particular. The next morning Woodfall repeated it word for word to Mr Cawthorn, who, capable of appreciating such rare talent, was so affected as to burst into tears" [20].

In later life, William Woodfall, as editor and reporter for the *Morning Chronicle*, would go on to develop an enviable reputation as the "father of parliamentary reporting", sitting for hours in the Chamber of the House of Commons listening to debates in a time when note taking was not allowed. He would then return to his office and reproduce the debates word perfect for the next edition of the *Chronicle*. Unlike some of Woodfall's contemporaries at Tonbridge, Cawthorn's style of teaching would have suited the young bookseller's son very well and he would most likely have thrived under the conditions prevailing in the schoolroom at that time. The reputation he developed would also have impressed his classmates, and in turn, their parents alike, which would have been of benefit to both the Woodfall family and also to James Cawthorn. For the headmaster may indeed have been the contributor to the *Gentleman's Magazine* who publically praised Henry Fielding's "base novel" published by the booksellers of London, but he could also attract young men of outstanding talent from this same community of literati to be educated in the school room at Tonbridge. Far from ritually humiliating William Woodfall, Cawthorn instead offers him a platform to display his unique gifts of nature, to the benefit of both pupil and Master.

On the other hand, his involvement with Robert Dodsley during the incubation of his *Tragedy of Cleone*, demonstrates the discretion that Cawthorn was also capable of displaying when dealing with this constituency with whom Cawthorn had a particular affiliation. The correspondence between the two men was a private matter.

Cawthorn needed the booksellers in order to help him realise his vision of establishing a library at Tonbridge and his relationship with them is both sensitive and measured. Promoting the cause of the booksellers was to promote Cawthorn's own interests, whereas avoiding being drawn into feuds amongst the literati was a sensible and calculated strategy. When viewed in the context of the development of the Cawthorn Library, James Cawthorn's nurturing of his literary connections, although overlooked by Hart, is both obvious and understandable, whilst also reflecting the seemingly contradictory character of the man.

Cawthorn's relationship with the Skinners also becomes clear when considered in light of his vision for Tonbridge School. Although he is undoubtedly deferential and obedient, particularly in the earlier part of his career as headmaster, Cawthorn is also clearly a man of determination. It is apparent that he was intent on succeeding where his predecessors had failed and Tonbridge School would get its first school library building during his tenure as headmaster. To this end he takes on the burden of personally underwriting the financial risk of the project, almost immediately when he finds himself in a position to do so, after the death of his father. This somewhat proprietorial approach as headmaster is not entirely welcomed by all of the Skinners' Company and results in a more uncomfortable, but nevertheless productive relationship between employer and employee.

The headmaster was also a man of principle and this was most clearly demonstrated by his refusal to abandon George Austen after the financial inquisition that followed the Sandhills debacle. Cawthorn was prepared to use the power vested in him through the school statutes to defy the

Skinners' Company and continue to pay Austen the salary due to the school Usher even when he was not actually in residence at Tonbridge. In standing by his former pupil, protégé and partner in the foundation of the Cawthorn Library, the headmaster ensured that the young Austen would continue to receive the financial support he needed in order to complete his studies at Oxford. Cawthorn practised what he preached: in order to be Great, one first had to be Good.

And what of George Austen, the "poor orphan"?

Traumatised at the age of six by the loss of his father, abandoned by his stepmother and sent to live with his Uncle Stephen, a bookseller in London for whom he most likely had to "mind the shop" before he was eventually sent back to school in Tonbridge. Surely, the demonic headmaster depicted in most histories of the school would have been the final straw that would have left the poor boy emotionally scarred for life. Instead he finds, "patient discipline and sound instruction" [21] from a headmaster who had also spent his earliest formative years "minding a bookshop", albeit in markedly different circumstances. His master and mentor had an obsessive love of books and enviable connections to the literary trade; he had a father-in-law with masonic connections to William Hogarth; a "worthy friend" who published books for the likes of Samuel Johnson; and of course, for the future father of Jane Austen, in a literary world dominated by men, what better education could Tonbridge School provide than by a tutor whose earliest literary influences came from one of the pre-eminent female novelists of the time, Eliza Haywood?

Barry Orchard suggests that,

> "It is hard to think of such a man as being as bad as other histories have painted him" [22].

Indeed it is, for if he was, it would be difficult to understand why George Austen returned to the school on his graduation from Oxford in order to become Cawthorn's deputy.

In fact, he returned in the summer of 1754, the year in which Thomas Cawthorn died, resulting in the sale of his interest in the lead mines in Yorkshire. Austen was employed as Usher, or assistant master, to Cawthorn during the actual construction of the library building and the increase in the number of "literary boys" attending the school. He would also have been, in his role as Cawthorn's deputy, most likely responsible for administering disciplinary fines and as such, George Austen played a significant supporting role in the establishment of the first library built at Tonbridge School.

The historical evidence suggests that Austen unambiguously resigned his post as Usher at Tonbridge only after the death of his master and mentor in 1761. He returned to reside permanently at St John's College in Oxford until in 1764 he married Cassandra Leigh. The couple's first child, a boy, was born a year later. George and Cassandra decided not to follow the traditional path of christening their first-born son after his father or one of his grandfathers, but instead chose another name for him. He was christened James.

James Cawthorn was the headmaster who built the

first library at Tonbridge School. The Cawthorn Library is also what defined the headmaster who built it.

The Fate of Cawthorn's Library...

In the mid nineteenth century, a hundred years after Cawthorn's library was built, the coming of the railways transformed the finances of both the Skinners' Company and Tonbridge School. The Sandhills Estate to the north of the Foundling Hospital was developed, with some of the land finally being sold. The purchaser, however, rather than being the home for abandoned children, the Foundling Hospital, was instead the Midlands Railway Company which,

> "... acquired compulsory powers to buy this land at a handsome price from the Skinners' Company"[23].

The land, forming part of the Sandhills Estate, purchased from the Skinners, was then used to build St Pancras Station. Ironically, in many respects, part of the proceeds from the sale of the Sandhills Estate were spent on redeveloping and extending the building that Cawthorn had originally built and the name was changed to the Skinners' Library. The link between Cawthorn and his library was therefore broken.

James Cawthorn's name has, however, to this day continued to be associated with a disciplinarian culture and tales of his ghost stalking the corridors on the anniversary of his death still keep the first-year Novi on their toes as they settle into school life at Tonbridge.

... and of the Schoolboy who killed another boy

Finally, as for the curious case of the schoolboy who was killed in an argument over a slice of cake; William Chetwynd was eventually found guilty of the manslaughter of Thomas Ricketts after a schoolboy quarrel, rather than the more serious charge of murder. His hand was burned in recognition of his crime, but he regained his liberty.

Perhaps it is time to free Cawthorn's ghost.

Notes and References

Abbreviations

CCEd – The Clergy of the Church of England database
FHA – Foundling Hospital Archives
GM – Gentleman's Magazine
LM – London Magazine and Monthly Chronologer
SCB – Skinners' Court Book
SCLP – Skinners' Company Ledger of Payments
SCLR – Skinners' Company Ledger of Receipts

Preface

1. Throughout the Skinners' Court records, and in a number of Tonbridge School references to James Cawthorn, his surname is usually spelt with the letter "e". For example; The Cawthorne Lecture Theatre at Tonbridge School. In reality however, this branch of the Cawthorne family usually spelt their surname without the "e", that is: Cawthorn. Most Cawthorn(e) families originate from the village of Cawthorne in the West Riding of Yorkshire. The original settlement from which the village derives its name was a Saxon

settlement, first mentioned in the Domesday Book. Hence the name is derived from a Saxon place name and there are a number of derivations of the spelling. When quoting source material this book uses the spelling as it appears in the original source.

2. Orchard, 1991 – p19

Chapter One

1. The transcript of the trial is available on "Old Bailey Proceedings on-line: Trial of William Chetwynd, Oct 1743". "Tim Hitchcock, Robert Shoemaker, Clive Emsley, Sharon Howard and Jamie Mchaughlin et al, The Old Bailey Proceedings Online, 1674-1913' (www.oldbaileyonline.org version 7.0, 24 March 2012).
2. Old Bailey on-line – Chetwynd 1743
3. ibid
4. Hans, – p87
5. Hans, – p87
6. Clare, – 1720
7. Clare, –1735
8. Hans, – p88
9. GM Vol 13. Oct 1743 p551
10. LM – Oct 1743 p516
11. LM – Dec 1743 p618
12. LM – Jan 1744 p48
13. The *Newgate Chronicles* or *Newgate Calendars* were originally a series of "flysheets" sold for a penny each and distributed in the streets. They typically described in lurid detail particularly scandalous or prominent

court cases of the times. A number of authors collected samples of the flysheets and reproduced them as books or compendiums. William Chetwynd's case appears, for example, in *Newgate Calendar* – Knapp and Baldwin, 1826.
14. Mullan, – ODNB
15. Clare, – 1740
16. Baggs, et al – pp51-57
17. PRO 30/21/3/1
18. CCEd – James Cawthorn: Person ID 724. DN/ORR/2/1
19. SCB9 – p408
20. SCB9 – p411
21. Cawthorn, – 1771 – pp200-201
22. Williams, 1913 – p185
23. Rivington, 1919 – p77
24. GM – Dec 1750 – p603
25. Brown, 1739
26. Wilson, 2001 – p30
27. Hans, 1951 – p142
28. Hans, – p140
29. Philosophical Transactions – 1731
30. Boerhaave, 1742
31. Salmon, 1744
32. Desaguliers, 1745 – Dr Desaguliers died in 1744 and the publication of this edition was organised by his son, Thomas Desaguliers.
33. London Electoral History (on-line archive) Warmote Polls – Castle Baynard 7th Jan 1740 – p106 Table 8.3.10.7 Source: *London Daily Post* – Dec 1739. Austen is only identified by his surname. Land

Registry records show Stephen Austen living in Castle Baynard between 1738 and 1741.
34. Tonbridge School Archives
35. Nokes, 1998 – p19 nb. Nokes quotes from Austen archives.
36. Le Faye, 2004 – p4
37. Hart, 1935 – p62
38. SCB9 – p421
39. SCB9 – p421
40. SCB9 – p426
41. SCB9 – p427
42. SCB9 – p427
43. SCB9 – p427
44. SCB9 – p427
45. SCB9 – p428
46. SCB9 – p430
47. SCB9 – p430
48. SCB9 – p430
49. SCB9 – p431
50. Knapp & Baldwin, 1826 – p77
51. ibid – p77
52. Hart, 1935 – pp65-66

Chapter Two

1. Rivington, 1869 – pp118-119
2. Somervell, 1947 – pp29-30
3. Orchard, 1991 – p18
4. ibid – p18
5. ibid – p19

6. ibid – p19
7. Rivington, 1869 – p119
8. SBC12 – p4
9. *London Chronicle*, April 1761.
10. Somervell – p30

Chapter Three

1. Stam – p316 – Section by Michael Meredith
2. Stam – p316 ibid
3. Rivington, 1869 – p53
4. Hoole *A Tonbridge Miscellany – Tonbridge School Library 1553-1962*, written for the opening of the Smythe Library, November 1962 – p1
5. ibid – p1
6. ibid – p1
7. ibid – p1
8. ibid – p2
9. ibid – p2
10. ibid – p1 – Spencer's Library Subscription Roll is dated 1729, and may have been a rather underwhelming response to the opening of the new Rowland Library at Eton.
11. ibid – p1 – A copy of this catalogue is held in Tonbridge School Archives.
12. From a collection of miscellaneous letters of John Fuller, held by the East Sussex Records Office. Ref: ESRO SAS/RF 15/25 folio 167v. The letter is addressed from Rosehill, the 26th July 1743. The John Lade referred to is actually the son of John Inskip and is the great-nephew of Sir

John Lade, Bart of Warbleton, Sussex. He succeeded to the estates of his great-uncle and thereupon took the name of Lade in 1740 – Hart pp159-160.
13. SCB 11 – p333
14. SCB 9 – pp461-464
15. SCB 9 – p462
16. SCB 9 –p 463
17. SCB 9 – p463
18. SCB 9 – p463
19. SCB 9 – p464
20. SCB 9 – p464
21. Oxford Alumni
22. Oxford Alumni
23. Cambridge Alumni
24. SCB 9 p530. It is noted that at a Court of Assistants Meeting held on the 1st August 1745 "… Mr Thomas Cawthorn, a hardwareman at Aldgate be… admitted into the Freedom of this Company by Redemption upon paying the usual fees". Interestingly however, there is no record of Thomas Cawthorn being admitted to the Freedom in the Freedom Registers of the Company (MS 30719/4), nor is there any record in the Register of Receipts (MS 30728/4) of a Thomas Cawthorn paying any Freedom fees. There are, however, later records of Thomas' younger brother Charles Cawthorn being apprenticed to Thomas, and in such records Thomas is described as a "… Citizen and Skinner of London" (MS 30719/4 – p45).
25. Cawthorn – 1745
26. This quote appears in the *Tonbridge Historical Society Newsletter,* Autumn 2011 and is taken from

the correspondence and papers of the Weller family of Chauntlers, held by the Kent Archives Office in Maidstone (ref: U1000/18).
27. CCEd – Johnson Towers: Person ID 2522
28. Cawthorn – 1771 – pp22-36
29. ibid – pp24-25
30. ibid – pp35-36
31. Le Faye – p4
32. SCB 9 – p610
33. SCB 9 – p617
34. The "window tax" was a property tax based on the number of windows in a property and was first introduced in 1696 under William III. In 1747 the tax was amended such that different rates were applied to properties in different bands, with a property placed into a particular band dependent upon the number of windows in the property. Obviously, by "bricking up" some windows, a property could be moved into a lower band and the amount of tax applicable would fall accordingly. The tax was always particularly unpopular as it was seen as a tax on "light and air". It was not, however, repealed until 1851.
35. The fellowship in question was a "White Fellowship" and was established by Sir Thomas White, Founder of St John's College, Oxford who was a great friend of Sir Andrew Judd, Founder of Tonbridge School. Rivington quotes an extract from Sir Thomas White's statutes of St John's, Oxford in which he gives particulars of the scholarships established, two each for schools in Coventry, Bristol and Reading and one for Tonbridge "… in respect of great love we did bear

Andrew Judd, Knighte, builder of the grammar school there... " Rivington, pp27-29.

36. GM 1791 – Rev. Edward Goodwin
37. SCLP3 – The Ledger of Payments shows that in June 1747 a fee was paid "to the Rev. Breadfrock who preached for Mr Cawthorne". The following year the fee is shown as being paid to the "Rev. James Cawthorne". Clearly, Cawthorn had been due to give his sermon in 1747 but after the death of his wife and daughter he was unable to do so, and he instead delivered his sermon the following year.
38. Chalmers, 1812 – p501
39. Lambeth Palace Library Archives. Papers of Archbishop Dr John Potter – Entry in Archbishop's Register – p244
40. Potter, 1724
41. Hart, School Rolls, p74
42. Royal Hospital, Chelsea Archives – LDRHC/16/0162.1
43. See Hart p150. See also Dean p310. – Dean gives Ashburnham's appointment as Sept 1737. There are, however, indications that he was in residence at Royal Hospital, Chelsea (RHC) prior to his official appointment. The Paymaster General was responsible for the payment of Army Pensions and these were administered through RHC. The Paymaster General at this time was Henry Pelham whose father, Sir Thomas Pelham, was educated at Tonbridge. There are a number of Tonbridge links to RHC during Pelham's tenure as Paymaster General.
44. Hart – p72

45. St Peter's and St Paul's Church, Tonbridge
46. CCEd – James Cawthorn: Person ID 724, Record ID 17994
47. Goodwin, GM 1791
48. Hunter – p98 and Goodall – p256
49. Mary Laughton had connections to Sheffield. Her father had a younger brother, Henry Laughton who fell on hard times and his two daughters – Mary's cousins – moved to Sheffield where they were taken under the patronage of a formidable local dowager Mrs Elizabeth Parkin, also known as "Madam" Parkin;

"Madam Parkin... with a fortune inherited from commerce... took under her especial patronage two young ladies, the Misses Laughton, daughters of a Lincolnshire gentleman, whose reduced circumstances were not quite on a level with their aristocratic claims. They brought with them a standard of elegance hitherto absent, and Mr Hunter (ie: Joseph Hunter – History of Hallamshire, etc) expressed the opinion that 'the settlement of these two accomplished young ladies in Sheffield had probably no small influence in producing the refinement in manners which was perceptible in several ladies of the better condition, in the generation that succeeded them'". Leader, p114

In due course, both of these Laughton cousins married into wealthy Sheffield families. The eldest, who like James Cawthorn's mother, was also called Mary, married Madam Parkin's heir, Walter Oborne, who inherited the Parkin fortune. The younger sister,

Elizabeth, married John Fell of Attercliffe Forge, and after his death in 1762 inherited his estate at New Hall, where she became known as "quite the Lady bountiful of the neighbourhood". Leader, pp114-115

50. Leader, p314
51. The year of birth of the children who survived into adulthood: Elizabeth – 1717; James – 1719; Thomas – 1723; Charles – 1729; Mary – 1731 and Sarah – 1733. Sheffield Parish Records.
52. Goodwin, GM 1791
53. CCEd – James Cawthorn; Person ID 724. Clare College, Cambridge archives.
54. Rivington, 1869 – p117
55. Cawthorn, 1771 – Poem is *Wit and Learning* – p198. The 'Wilcox' most likely refers to Dr John Wilcox, Master of Clare Hall 1736 – 1762.
56. Rivington, 1869 – p50
57. Cawthorn, 1771 – poem is *The Lottery – Inscribed to Miss H…* p93
58. ibid – p93
59. Leader, p314. In Chancery Court Papers C/11/2295/64 he is referred to as "Upholsterer".
60. Campbell, pp169-170
61. ibid p332
62. ibid p340
63. Orchard, p20
64. There are a number of accounts of the Wardlow Moor mine venture. The original Chancery Court papers are held at the National Archives, Kew; "Thomas Cawthorn and others in Sheffield – Litigation 1729" ref: C11/496/24. These original court transcripts name

one of Thomas Cawthorn's partners in the venture as George Steer. An account of the mine and the litigation surrounding it is also included in Longstone Records, Derbyshire by G.T. Wright, JP published in Bakewell, Derbyshire by Benjamin Gratton, Printer – 1906. This account quotes *The Compleat Mineral Law...* (see below) and prior to doing so, attributes the book to George Steer – "Written on the fly leaf are the words – 'Compiled by George Steer'". Page 342 of Longstone Records.

65. C11/496/24
66. *The Compleat Mineral Laws of Derbyshire,* taken from the originals, attributed by both G.T. Wright (see above) and the British Library to George Steer. Printed by Henry Woodfall; and sold by Richard Williamson, at Gray's Inn Gate in Holborn; John Haxby, bookseller in Sheffield and by Job Bradley, bookseller in Chesterfield, 1734. This compilation of laws and customs covering the Peak District quotes a number of mine trials as examples in order to illustrate particular points. One of the cases quoted is that of the mine on Wardlow Moor which Thomas Cawthorn and his partners lost as a result of what *The Compleat Mineral Laws...* describes as "two sham trials" p52. Interestingly, in *The Compleat Mineral Laws...* one of Thomas Cawthorn's partners is named as "John Steer" despite very clearly being recorded as "George Steer" in the original court papers. This would appear to be an attempt by the author of the book, George Steer, to distance himself from the obvious charge of a "conflict of interest" in giving such a one-sided

account of a trial in which he appears to be one of the losing plaintiffs.

67. This quote is taken from the original Chancery Division court case documents held at the National Archives, Kew; "Thomas Cawthorne – Upholsterer, et al... Litigation, Farming". Ref: C/11/2295/64. The reference to "Farming" in the title is misleading, for although the court case centres around what is undoubtedly "farmland", a reading of the proceedings highlights the fact that the dispute is really about "mining access rights" for a seam of lead ore that runs beneath the farmland in question.

68. For a description of the records from the English Civil War covering lead mining in this area, which is also known as "Bitholms", see *Handbook No.4 – The Early History of Stocksbridge and District... Lead Mining in the Ewden Valley*, by Joseph Kenworthy - p35. Published by Joseph Kenworthy – Stretton Villa, Deepcar near Sheffield, 1915.

69. C/11/2295/64 – The venture was originally divided into twenty-four shares, with each share entitled to "one dish of ore" from the mine. Thomas Cawthorn owned ten of the original shares and his brother John Cawthorn owned a single share. The landowner, Nicholas Stead, owned four shares and his father, Thomas Stead, owned a single share. Four other Sheffield "adventurers" owned the remaining shares between them.

70. The landowners were effectively paid a royalty in the form of a minority share of the lead produced from the mine. After every twelve dishes of ore were produced

from the mine, a thirteenth dish was allocated to these adjacent landowners, beneath whose property the ore body extended. Revenue from the sale of this thirteenth dish was divided between the relevant landowners.

71. The litigation stemmed from a dispute amongst the original investors. Nicholas Stead, the owner of the land on which the original ore deposit was discovered, appears to have sold his shares to new investors before trying to sue the consortium for "trespass" as a means of gaining control of the mine. His father, Thomas Stead, remained a part of the consortium and was one of the "adventurers" whom Nicholas tried to dispossess. The litigation appears to be the result of desperation on the part of Nicholas Stead which in turn was the result of serious financial difficulties he experienced as a result of debts he had accumulated in other ventures.
72. C/11/2295/64 – one of the later investors, who came into the mine venture by buying shares from one of the original investors once the mine was established, was Elizabeth "Madam" Parkin, guardian of Mary Laughton's (James's mother) cousins (see above).
73. The Last Will and Testament of Thomas Cawthorn of Sheffield. Proved the 4th May 1754. Held at National Archives, Kew – ref: PROB/11/808/211
74. ibid
75. ibid
76. Leader, p193
77. Leader, p193

Chapter Four

1. Goodwin, GM – 1791
2. Land Registry records held at the National Archives, Kew, show Thomas Cawthorn listed as the occupant of premises on Leadenhall Street, Aldgate, City of London from 1752 until his death in 1754. Charles Cawthorn then takes over the premises and is listed as the occupant until his death in 1772 at which point the property is listed under "Widow Cawthorn". This will be Anne Cawthorn (nee, Speller), second wife of Charles whom he married in 1766 after the death of his first wife, Elizabeth. Anne continued to live in the premises until the 1780s. She died in 1813, and her death was reported in the *Gentleman's Magazine* Vol 83, Part 1 p93 under deaths – "Jan 19th. In Whitechapel, aged 82, Mrs Ann Cawthorn, relic of the late Chas. C. of Leadenhall Street, hardwareman". The property at 88 Leadenhall Street (see Baldwins) was a short distance from the Offices of the East India Company. Leadenhall Market was a natural district for Thomas and Charles Cawthorn to establish their businesses because since 1622 it had the exclusive rights to sell cutlery in London. For two young men from Yorkshire with cousins who were Hallamshire Cutlers, it made sense to establish their businesses close to the centre of the cutlery trade in London. Charles' son, also called Thomas, born to his first wife and baptised at St Katherine's Cree, Leadenhall Street on the 14th Dec 1757, is not listed as the registered occupant at any point. This Thomas was most likely

the Cawthorn who is listed in Hart, p86 as being in the 4th Class at Tonbridge School in 1770, during Johnson Towers' tenure as headmaster. Unfortunately, the school records are very incomplete for this period and it is impossible to calculate how long Thomas Jnr, James Cawthorn's nephew, was at Tonbridge.

3. SCB 11, p112. Although there are no records in either the Freedom Register or the Ledger of Receipts suggesting that James' brother Thomas had confirmed his membership of the Worshipful Company of Skinners, this is not the case for his younger brother. Charles had originally gained his freedom in 1752 as evidenced by the following entry in the Skinners Freedom Register for the 7th July 1752 "… Charles Cawthorn, son of Thomas Cawthorn of Sheffield in the County of York, Upholder, Apprenticed to Thomas Cawthorn, Citizen and Skinner (sic) of London for Seven Years… Memdum nothing paid" (MS 30719/4 p45). It is also noted in the Skinners' Ledger of Receipts(MS 30728/4 p293) that Charles is soon also admitted to the Livery of the Company when the following entry for the 22nd July 1757 is recorded, "… Mr Charles Cawthorne, For his Fine for being admitted on the Livery, £15 – Paid in Full".

4. SCB 13 – p70 June 1772. Being elected "Renter Warden" was usually the first step on the path to becoming Master of the Company but unfortunately, Charles's untimely death at the age of forty-four in the following year denied him the opportunity of achieving such heights.

5. SCB 11, p127

6. SCB 11, p128
7. SCB 11, p128
8. SCB 11, p177
9. In the nineteenth century, the library was enlarged and extended, and Knox, the headmaster at that time "... pleaded that 'the present noble library, finished in the Grecian style of architecture', should be left alone" – Hoole, p2.
10. SCB 11, p177
11. SCB 11, p202
12. GM, Goodwin, 1791 pp1081-1083
13. Cawthorn, 1771 – *Of Taste – An Essay* pp114-115
14. ibid, pp115-116
15. ibid, p116, p119
16. Foundling Hospital Archives, held at the London Metropolitan Archives. A/FH/A/3/2/4 – meeting held on April 7th 1756
17. Daily Advertiser – No. 7908 – the 18th May 1756
18. Rivington, 1869 – p117
19. Cawthorn, 1771 pp128-129. Poem *Life Unhappy, Because We Use It Improperly – A Moral Essay* – recited at the visitation of 1760 by the Head Boy, James Thurston. Handel died in April 1759 and Cawthorn clearly lamented his loss.
20. Foundling Hospital Records: A/FH/A/3/2/4 – Meeting held on the 21st May 1756
21. ibid – Meeting held on the 24th May 1756
22. ibid – Meeting held on the 14th July 1756
23. SCB 11, p205
24. This point is noted in the minutes of the Court of Assistants meeting held on the 15th July 1756 – SCB

11, p205 – and is repeated in a Foundling Hospital Meeting held on the 4th August 1756 – A/FH/A/3/2/4.
25. SCB 11, p207
26. SCB 11, p208
27. SCB 11, p209
28. SCB 11, p213
29. SCB 11, p213
30. Foundling Hospital Records – A/FH/A/3/2/4 – Meeting held on the 27th October 1756
31. ibid
32. ibid
33. ibid
34. SCB 11, p216
35. Foundling Hospital Records: A/FH/A/3/2/5
36. ibid – Meeting held on the 26th January 1757
37. ibid – Meeting held on the 13th December 1756
38. SCB 11, p221 – The meeting was chaired by Alderman Kite, Master of the Company. Also in attendance was Sir Charles Asgill.
39. SCB 11, p222
40. SCB 11, p393
41. Hart pp46-47 and also p150

Chapter Five

1. Goodwin, GM 1791
2. Chalmers, 1810, p229
3. ibid, p229
4. Haywood, 1726
5. *Dictionary of Literary Biography* – Volume 154.

Section by Michael Treadwell, pp248-249
6. Leader, p130
7. ibid, p130
8. ibid, p130
9. Mullan, ODNB
10. ibid
11. Haywood, 1732
12. Cawthorn, J – PROB/11/865/162 – National Archives, Kew, London
13. ibid
14. Johnson, 1735
15. Johnson, 1755 – Johnson's *Dictionary of the English Language* was originally commissioned in 1747 by a consortium of eight leading booksellers; Charles Hitch – Cawthorn's "worthy friend"; Andrew Millar; Robert and his brother, James Dodsley; Thomas and his son, Thomas Longman; James and his son, Paul Knapton. Like Charles Hitch (apprenticed from 1718), Paul Knapton (from 1721) had been apprenticed to Arthur Bettesworth. Another of Bettesworth's apprentices, John Hinton (from 1732) later married Stephen Austen's widow, Elizabeth on the 10th August 1752, after Stephen's death in December 1751.
16. Goodwin, GM – 1791, p1081
17. Johnson, 1738
18. Hart, p10
19. ibid, pp10-11
20. Roberts, p101
21. GM, Aug 1749, p371
22. ibid
23. The book commissioned from Richardson by Charles

Rivington and John Osborn was published later in 1740 under the title *Letters written to and for particular Friends, on the most important Occasions. Directing not only the requisite Style and Forms, to be observed in writing Familiar Letters; but how to think and act justly and prudently in the common Concerns of Human Life.* The book contained anecdotes and lessons on how a person should live their life and ran to six editions during Richardson's lifetime.

24. Richardson, 1740
25. Haywood, 1741
26. Fielding, 1741
27. Keymer, 2005
28. Cawthorn, 1745
29. GM, Oct 1749
30. Hart, p10
31. ibid, p10
32. ibid, p11
33. Leader, p120
34. SCB 9, p530 – Thomas Cawthorn is made a Freeman of the Skinners' Company – 1745.
35. Cawthorn, 1771 – The poem is *Wit and Learning – An Allegory* and the reference is again interesting when viewed in the context of Cawthorn's life. Unlike the learned and serious character, "Learning", who "often call'd in at Hitch's shop", the other character in the poem is the more jovial and less serious "Wit" who;

"... left the law, and all its drudges,
With curses, to my lords the judges,

Call'd for a coach, and went to dwell
At Robin (sic) Dodsleys in Pall-Mall"

36. Tierney, p12
37. Soloman, pp212-213
38. Tierney, p271
39. ibid, p271
40. ibid, p272
41. Hart, p6

Chapter Six

1. Clare, M and Barwis, C – 1744-1751
2. Hans, p89
3. PRO/30/21/3/1
4. Rivington, 1869 - p116
5. Clare, M and Barwis, C, p2
6. ibid, p2
7. ibid, p3
8. ibid, p4
9. ibid, p4
10. ibid, p4
11. ibid, p4
12. ibid, p5
13. ibid, p5
14. ibid, p5
15. ibid, p5
16. ibid, p5
17. ibid, p5
18. ibid, p5

19. ibid, p5
20. ibid, p6
21. ibid, p6
22. ibid, p6
23. ibid, p6
24. ibid, p6
25. Hans, p89
26. Hart, p10
27. A number of Parliamentary inquiries were held after the South Sea Bubble burst, when the activities of the directors in particular came in for scrutiny. The evidence presented at the time is held in the Parliamentary Archives and makes interesting reading. Some of the evidence presented shows the activity of agents who sometimes acted for directors in their personal dealings in South Sea Company stock. Their dealings on behalf of other investors, often appears on the same pages of the accounts they submitted for scrutiny. Sampson Gideon's name appears on a number of these accounts, particularly on the "3rd Money Subscription" pages for 1719 and 1720. He was clearly an active trader in the Company's shares.
28. Nicholls, p642
29. Cawthorn, 1771, pp129-140
30. ibid, p129
31. Letter to George Montagu – 21st October 1959. See Middleton, 2002, p146. See also Toynbee, 1903, p314.
32. Somervell, pp32-33
33. Rivington, 1869 - p118
34. Hart, p10

35. Goodwin, GM, 1791, p1082
36. Nokes, p19
37. SCB 9, p464
38. Rivington, 1869 – p117

Chapter Seven

1. Orchard, p18
2. SCB 12, p13
3. Rivington, 1869 – p56
4. SCB 9, pp430-431
5. SCB 12, p20
6. SCB 12, p26
7. SCB 12, p29
8. SCB 12, p29
9. SCB 12, p54
10. Hoole, p2
11. In the eighteenth century, a significant number of books were printed by subscription and the names of the subscribers were usually included in the front of the book. The *Rev. James Cawthorn – headmaster of Tunbridge School* appears on numerous occasions in books printed during his tenure as Headmaster of Tonbridge School. In theory, it may be possible to recreate Cawthorn's library book legacy by cataloguing all the books in which his name appears amongst the list of subscribers. However, discussions with the British Library would suggest that this is a virtually impossible task. Every edition, of every book, published by every publisher/bookseller during the twenty years of Cawthorn's tenure as headmaster

would need to be checked and this alone would be a herculean task. It would also not account for those books bought subsequently by Cawthorn where his name does not appear amongst the original subscribers. Lewis and Winterton were unable to complete the catalogue in 1761 despite spending over twelve months on their attempt, such was the scale of the task, and it would be infinitely more difficult to attempt it today.
12. PROB/11/865/162
13. Leader, p193
14. GM Vol 31, May 1761, p232
15. Southam, p293

Chapter Eight

1. Hart, p62
2. SCB 9, pp461-464
3. Oxford Alumni.
4. The Sir Thomas White Fellowship paid a modest stipend of 2s 6d per term – St John's College, Oxford archives.
5. St John's College, Oxford archives.
6. Austen received a Paddy Exhibition and was also an Assistant Reader in Logic in 1751 – St John's College, Oxford archives.
7. The Sir Thomas White Fellowship stipend increased to 4s per term – St John's College, Oxford archives.
8. Register of Absences Book, St John's College, Oxford archives.

9. Austen was awarded a Barker Exhibition in 1753 – St John's College, Oxford archives.
10. Austen was awarded a Paddy Exhibition in 1754 – St John's College, Oxford archives.
11. SCB 11, p256
12. ibid
13. Register of Absences Book, St John's College, Oxford archives.
14. SCB 11, p256
15. SCB 9, p461
16. ibid
17. SCB 9, p563
18. SCLP 3, p78
19. Rivington, 1869 – p49
20. SCLP 3, p92
21. SCLP 3, pp156-157
22. SCLP 3, p157
23. SCLP 3, p157 and p231
24. SCB 11, p177
25. Register of Absences Book, St John's College, Oxford archives.
26. SCB 11, pp221-222
27. SCB 11, p148
28. SCB 11, p231
29. SCB 11, pp237-238
30. SCB 11, p238
31. SCB 11, p239
32. ibid
33. ibid
34. SCB 11, p307
35. SCB 12, p11

36. ibid
37. SCB 12, p13
38. Southam, p290
39. ibid, p291
40. ibid, p291
41. CCEd – record ID 16780
42. CCEd – Person ID 724, Record ID 17994
43. SCLP 3, p157
44. CCEd – George Austen; Person ID 133, Record ID 257499. Henry Austen; Person ID 69334, Record ID 256836

Chapter Nine

1. SCB 12, p7 – Court of Assistants Meeting held on the 29th April 1761 at which "the Office or place of Schoolmaster was conferred upon the said Mr Towers..."
2. Hart, p7
3. Orchard, p19
4. Orchard, p21
5. Le Faye, p4
6. Le Faye, p4
7. Rivington, 1869, p119

Chapter Ten

1. Rivington, 1869, p117
2. Hart, p170 – The quote is taken from *Publishing Family of Rivington*, p 112, Septimus Rivington, published by Rivington's in 1919

3. Hart, p170
4. Somervell, p29
5. Chalmers, 1812
6. Chalmers, 1810
7. Chalmers, 1810, p230
8. ibid, p230
9. ibid, p230
10. ibid, p230
11. Johnson, 1790
12. Cawthorn, 1771
13. Johnson, 1790, p6
14. ibid, p6
15. Goodwin, GM Dec 1791, pp1081-1083
16. ibid
17. ibid
18. Cawthorn, 1771, pp209-210
19. Orchard, p18
20. Rivington, 1869, pp119-120
21. Nokes, p19
22. Orchard, p18
23. Somervell, p59

BIBLIOGRAPHY

Unpublished Sources

Cawthorn, James – *Last Will and Testament*, National Archives, Kew, London. PROB/11/865/162

Cawthorn, Thomas – *Last Will and Testament*, National Archives, Kew, London. PROB/11/808/211

Chancery Court Papers - *Cawthorn, Thomas and others, Sheffield – Litigation – 1729* – National Archives, Kew, London. C11/496/24

Chancery Court Papers – *Cawthorne, Thomas – Upholsterer, et al – Litigation – 1735*. National Archives, Kew, London. C/11/2295/64

Clergy of the Church of England database 1540-1835 – online record www.theclergydatabase.org.uk

Foundling Hospital Archives – London Metropolitan Archives office, London. A/FH/A/3/2/4 and A/FH/A/3/2/5.

Fuller, John – *Miscellaneous Letters* – East Sussex Record Office. ESRO SAS/RF 15/25 folio 167v.

Lambeth Palace Archives – *Papers of Archbishop Dr John Potter.*

London Electoral History 1700-1850 in www.Londonelectoralhistory.com

Ordination Register – Thomas Gooch, Bishop of Norwich – St Margaret's, Westminster. NRO, DN/ORR/2/1

Parliamentary Archives, South Sea Company investigations, Subscription Lists. Houses of Parliament, London. HL/PO/JO/10/2/158 and HL/PO/JO/10/6/322

Register of Marriages and Baptisms, Parish of St Anne's, Westminster, Middlesex. National Archives, Kew, London. PRO 30/21/3/1

Royal Hospital, Chelsea Archives – LDRHC/16/0162.1

Skinners' Court Book No.9 – 1733-1748 – MS 30708/9, Guildhall Library, London – Ancient Manuscripts Section (SCB9).

Skinners' Court Book No.10 – 1748-1752 – MS 30708/10, Guildhall Library, London – Ancient Manuscripts Section (SCB10).

Skinners' Court Book No.11 – 1752-1761 – MS 30708/11, Guildhall Library, London – Ancient Manuscripts Section (SCB11).

Skinners' Court Book No.12 – 1761-1770 – MS 30708/12, Guildhall Library, London – Ancient Manuscripts Section (SCB12).

Skinners' Court Book No.13 – 1770-1780 – MS 30708/13, Guildhall Library, London – Ancient Manuscripts Section (SCB13).

Skinners' Court Book No.14 – 1780-1789 – MS 30708/14, Guildhall Library, London – Ancient Manuscripts Section (SCB14).

Skinners' Company Freedom Register 1724-1764 – MS 30719/4, Guildhall Library, London – Ancient Manuscripts Section (SCFR4).

Skinners' Company Ledger of Payments – 1722-1745 – MS 30729/2, Guildhall Library, London – Ancient Manuscripts Section (SCLP2).

Skinners' Company Ledger of Payments – 1745-1787 – MS 30729/3, Guildhall Library, London – Ancient Manuscripts Section (SCLP3).

Skinners' Company Ledger of Receipts – 1745-1775 – MS 30728/4, Guildhall Library, London – Ancient Manuscripts Section (SCLR4).

Tonbridge School Archives, Tonbridge

Published Sources

Baggs A.P., Bolton D.K., Croot P.E.C. – *"Islington Manors"* in *'A History of the County of Middlesex – Vol. 8 Islington and Stoke Newington Parishes'* (London 1985).

Baldwin, R. – *"Baldwins Complete Guide to All Persons Who Have Any Trade or Concern With the City of London and Parts Adjacent"* 12th Ed. (London, 1770).

Boerhaave, Herman – *Boerhaave's Aphorisms: concerning the Knowledge and Care of Diseases* (London, 1742).

Brown, Edward – *The Travels and Adventures of Edward Brown, Esq. Formerly a Merchant of London* (London, 1739).

Campbell, Robert – *The London Tradesman* (London, 1747).

Cawthorn, James – *A Sermon preached before the Worshipful Burgesses of Westminster at St Margaret's Church, April 18th 1745* (London, 1745).

Cawthorn, James – *Benevolence, the source and ornament of civil distinctions. A Sermon preached in St. Antholin's church; before The Worshipful Company of Skinners; upon Thursday the 9th June, 1748* (London, 1748).

Cawthorn, James – *Poems, By The Rev. Mr. Cawthorn, Late Master of Tunbridge School* (London, 1771).

Chalmers, Alexander – *The Works of the English Poets from Chaucer to Cowper with Prefaces Biographical and Critical by Dr Samuel Johnson and the Most Approved Translation. The Additional Lives by Alexander Chalmers, FSA – Vol. 14* (London, 1810).

Chalmers, Alexander – *The General Biographical Dictionary containing an Historical and Critical Account of the Writings of the Most Eminent Persons in every Nation, particularly the British and Irish, from the Earliest accounts to the Present Time* (London, 1812).

Clare, Martin – *Motion of Fluids* (London, 1735).

Clare, Martin – *Youth's Introduction to Trade and Business for the use of schools 1st Ed.* (London, 1720).

Clare, Martin – *Youth's Introduction to Trade and Business 5th Ed.* (London, 1740).

Clare, Martin and Barwis MA, Rev. Cuthbert – *Rules and Orders for the Government of the Academy in Soho Square* (London).

Dean, Capt. C. G. T. – *The Royal Hospital, Chelsea* (London, 1950).

Desaguliers, Dr John Theophilus – *A Course of Experimental Philosophy* (London, 1745).

Fielding, Henry – *An Apology for the Life of Mrs Shamela Andrews by Mr Conny Keyber* (London, 1741).

Fielding, Henry – *The History of Tom Jones – A Foundling* (London, 1749).

Goodall, Armitage – *Place Names of South West Yorkshire, that is, of so much of the West Riding as lies south of the Aire from Keighley onwards* (Cambridge, 1913).

Goodwin, Rev. Edward – *Original memories of the Rev. James Cawthorn* – GM, Dec 1791 pp1081-1083

Hans, Nicholas – *New Trends in Education in the Eighteenth Century* (London, 1951).

Hart, Walter Gray – *The Register of Tonbridge School from 1553 to 1820* (London, 1935).

Haywood, Eliza – *Memories of a Certain Island adjacent to the Kingdom of Utopia* (London, 1726).

Haywood, Eliza – *Secret Histories, Novels and Poems* (London, 1732).

Haywood, Eliza – *The Anti-Pamela; or Feign'd Innocence Detected* (London, 1741).

Hester, Rev. Giles – *James Cawthorne, The First Sheffield Poet.* Sheffield Miscellany (Sheffield, 1907).

Hoole, G.P. – *A Tonbridge Miscellany* (Tonbridge, 1985).

Hunter, Joseph – *Hallamshire – The History and Topography of the Parish of Sheffield in the County of York* (London, 1819).

Hunter, Joseph – *South Yorkshire, The History and Topography – Vol. 2* (London, 1831).

Johnson, Samuel – *A Voyage to Abyssinia by Father Jerome Lobo* (London, 1735).

Johnson, Samuel – *London, A Poem* (London, 1738).

Johnson, Samuel – *Dictionary of the English Language* (London, 1755).

Johnson, Samuel – *The Works of the English Poets, Vol. 65* (London, 1790).

Johnson, Samuel and Chalmers, Alexander – *The Works of the English Poets from Chaucer to Cowper with the Additional Lives by Alexander Chalmers FSA* (London, 1810). See Chalmers above.

Kenworthy, Joseph – *Handbook No.4 – The Early History of Stocksbridge and District... Lead Mining in the Ewden Valley* (Sheffield, 1915).

Keymer, Thomas – *Parliamentary Printing, Paper Credit and Corporate Fraud: A new Episode in Richardson's Early Career' – Eighteenth Century Fiction, Vol. 17 Issue 2 Article 3* (Toronto, 2005).

Knapp, Andrew and Baldwin, William – *Newgate Calendar* (London, 1826).

Leader, Robert Eadon – *Sheffield in the Eighteenth Century* (Sheffield, 1901).

Le Faye, Deirdre – *Jane Austen, A Family Record* (Cambridge, 2004).

Middleton, Richard – *The Bells of Victory: The Pitt-Newcastle Ministry and conduct of the Seven Years' War* (Cambridge, 2002).

Mullan, John – *Cawthorn, James (1719-1761), Oxford Dictionary of National Biography,* Oxford University Press (Oxford 2004). Online edn, Jan 2008.

Nichols, John – *Literary Anecdotes of the Eighteenth Century, Vol. IX* (London, 1815).

Nokes, David – *Jane Austen: A Life* (California, 1998).

Orchard, H. Barry. – *A Look at the Head and the Fifty* (London, 1991).

Philosophical Transactions – *The Journal of The Royal*

Society (London, 1731).

Potter, Dr John – *A Discourse on Church Government 3rd edition* (London, 1724).

Richardson, Samuel – *Letters Written to and for particular friends, on the most important Occasions* (London, 1740).

Richardson, Samuel – *Pamela: or Virtue Rewarded* (London, 1740).

Rivington, Septimus – *The History of Tonbridge School From Its Foundation to the Present Date* (London, 1869).

Rivington, Septimus – *The Publishing Family of Rivington* (London 1919).

Roberts, William – *Memoirs of the life and correspondence of Mrs Hannah More, Vol. 1* (New York, 1834).

Salmon, Thomas – *Modern History of the Present State of all Nations* (London, 1744).

Soloman, Harry M. – *The Rise of Robert Dodsley – Creating the New Age of Print* (Illinois, 1996).

Somervell, David C. – *A History of Tonbridge School* (London, 1947).

Southam, Brian – *George Austen: Pupil, Usher and Proctor* – Tonbridge Miscellany (Tonbridge, 2000).

Stam, David. H. – *International Dictionary of Library Histories* (New York, 2001).

Steer, George – *The Compleat Mineral Laws of Derbyshire, taken from the originals* (London, 1734).

Tierney, James E., - *The Correspondence of Robert Dodsley 1733-1764* (Cambridge, 2004).

Tonbridge Historical Society Newsletter – Autumn 2011 (Tonbridge, 2011).

Toynbee, Paget (ed.) – *The Letters of Horace Walpole, Fourth Earl of Oxford, Vol. IV* (Oxford, 1903).

Treadwell, Michael – *Dictionary of Literary Biography. Vol. 154* (Detroit, 1995).

Williams, Charles Francis Abdy – *Handel* (London, 1913).

Wilson, Margaret – *Jane Austen's family and Tonbridge* (Winchester, 2001).

Wright, G.T. – *Longstone Records, Derbyshire* (Bakewell, Derbyshire, 1906).

INDEX

Addison, Joseph 86
Annus Miribalis 117
Ashburnham, William 47
Asgill, Charles 83, 91
Atkinson, Rowland 143
Austen, Francis 141
Austen, George 11-13, 22, 38, 40-44, 62, 65, 119-121, 136-157, 165,183
Austen, Henry 12, 22, 91, 136, 160
Austen, James 183
Austen, Jane 182
Austen, John 9
Austen, Leonora 11-12
Austen, Philadelphia 11-12
Austen, Stephen 9-13, 40
Austen, Thomas 136, 161
Austen, William 11
Barnardiston, John 91
Barwis, Cuthbert 107-114
Bathurst, Richard 37, 39
Berenger, Jean 102
Bettesworth, Arthur 9-10, 88
Buckle, Henry 142
Bythams 56-58
Campbell, Robert 53-54
Cawthorn, Charles 60-61, 130
Cawthorn, Elizabeth 26-27, 50, 58, 85, 127-128, 132, 144, 154

Cawthorn, James 6, 8, 12-28, 33-52, 60-68, 77-78, 84-105, 115-138, 144, 156-185
Cawthorn, Mary (nee Laughton) 50, 132
Cawthorn, Mary 7, 44
Cawthorn, Richard 46
Cawthorn, Sarah 132
Cawthorn, Thomas Snr 6, 49, 52-59, 85-86, 143, 183
Cawthorn, Thomas Jnr 39, 60, 96, 100, 143
Cawthorne, village of 49
Cawthorne, Mary 136
Cawthorne, William 136
Chalmers, Alexander 45, 170-172
Chetwyn, William 1-2, 5, 21, 185
Chiddingstone, Village of 46, 133
Children, George 47
Children, John 47
Children, Richard 47-48
Clare Hall, Cambridge 39, 50-51, 89
Clare, Anne 107
Clare, Martin 2-8, 17, 30, 46, 56, 97, 107-114
Clare, Mary 7, 107
Congreve, William 86
Cooke, John 38
Cooper, Myles 155
Coram, Thomas 68
Corpus Christ, Cambridge 91
Cowper, William 136
Dalyson, Thomas 149-150
Dalyson, William 38
Defoe, Daniel 86
Desaguliers, Dr John Theophilus 3-4, 10
Dodsley, Robert 89, 101-104, 157, 180
Dolly's Chop House 8-9
Drury Lane Theatre 102, 104
St. Edmunds Hall, Oxford 39

Enlightenment, The 4, 170
Erwell, Elizabeth 117
Eton College 29-30, 125
Fayting, Nicholas 37, 39-40
Ferox Hall 47
Fielding, Henry 9, 86, 95-101, 157
Foundling Hospital 68-82, 146, 184
Frederick the Great 116
Freemasons 4, 10
Gainsborough, Thomas 68
Garrick, David 101-104
Gideon, Sampson Snr 115-119
Gideon, Sampson Jnr 115-119, 133-135
Goodwin, Edward Snr 174-177
Goodwin, Edward Jnr 58, 130
Gordon, Samuel 65
Graves, Richard 102
Great Fire of London 33
Hampton Court 46
Handel, George Frederic 9, 47, 69-70, 157
Hans, Nicholas 107, 114
Hart, Walter Gray 90-92, 104, 139-140
Hawksworth, John 102
Haywood, Eliza 85-86, 88, 97, 157, 182
Hitch, Charles Snr 8-11, 40, 88, 93, 97-98, 102-103
Hitch, Charles Jnr 93
Hitch, Paul 93
Hogarth, William 4, 47, 182
Hooper, Elizabeth 12
Humphreys, Hannah 2
Innys, William 10-11
Jacobite Rebellion 95, 116
Jonathan's Coffee House 115
Johnson, Samuel 86-89, 101, 172-174, 182
Judd, Sir Andrew 19, 30-33, 71, 73, 79, 143

Kelk, Suzanna 11
Kent, Henry 26
Kings Arms Masonic Lodge 4
Knight, Thomas 136
Knox, Vicesimus 130, 164-165
Lade, John 33
Laughton, Sir Edmund 50
Laughton, Edmund 50
Laughton, Mary 50
Lead Mining 54-59
Leader, Robert Eadon 86-87
Leigh, Cassandra 152, 183
Leigh, James 153
Leigh, village of 47-48, 158
Lewis, Joshua 126,129
Little Tower Street Academy 4, 10
Lord Mayor of London 82-83
Madras, Siege of 117
Mathews, Timothy 142
Midlands Railway Company 184
Minden, Battle of 117
Newton, George 37, 39
Onslow, Arthur 6, 56, 97
Onslow, George 6
Orchard, Barry 24-25, 124, 163, 178, 183
Oriel College, Oxford 39
Osborn, John 97
Pelham, Henry 115
Pope, Alexander 9, 86-88, 101, 157
Potter, Dr John 7, 45-46
Potter, John 45
Potter, Thomas 45
Prior, Matthew 86
Quebec City 117
Queen Anne 46

Queen Elizabeth I 73-74, 79
Queen's College, Cambridge 22, 136
Quiberon Bay, Battle of 117
Ramhurst Manor 47
Reynolds, Joshua 68
Richardson, Samuel 96-97
Ricketts, Thomas 1-6, 15-23, 27, 107-109, 185
Rivington, Charles 97
Rivington, Francis 94, 169-170
Rivington, John 10
Rivington, Septimus 23-25, 94, 117-118, 166, 169
Roberts, James 86-88
Roots, Thomas 7
Roubiliac, Louis Francois 47-48
Rowland, Thomas 29
Royal Hospital, Chelsea 47
Royal Society 4, 10
St. Johns Oxford 44-45, 137, 141-142, 147-149, 153, 158, 160, 165, 183
St. Pancras Station 185
St. Pauls School 93
Sampson, Mary 93
Sandhills Estate 71-82, 147, 152, 184
Sedgewick, Samuel 38-39
Seven Years War 116-117
Shenstone, William 102
Shipbourne 158
Silkstone 49
Smith, John 87
Smith, John Christopher Snr 9
Smith, John Christopher Jnr 9
Smith, John Pye 87
Smythe, Thomas 31, 141, 147-150, 158
Soho Academy 1-6, 20-21, 30, 89, 106-114
Somervell, David 24, 27, 170
South Sea Bubble 115

Southam, Brian 137, 156-157
Spencer, Richard 7, 11-20, 31-33, 85, 124
Stead, Nicholas 56
Steer, George 56-57
Stephens, Gilbert 14-18
Steventon 136, 161
Swift, Jonathan 9, 86
The Tea Table 85
Thurgoland 49
Thurston, James 116
Topham, Richard 30
Towers, John 40
Towers, Johnson 40, 61-62, 130, 143, 148, 159, 162-164
Tragedy of Cleone 102-104
Tully's Head 101
Unwin, Morley 136
Walpole, Horace 115, 117
Wardlow Moor 55-56
Walter, Rebecca 11
Walter, William 11
Wase, Christopher 31, 124
Watts, Thomas 10
Weller, Edward 40
Weller, Elizabeth 9, 47
Weller, Jane 47
Weller, Robert 9, 47
Westminster School 29, 125
White, Sir Thomas 45, 140, 148
Winchester School 29, 125
Window Tax 43-44
Wilcox, John 51
Winterton, John 126-130
Woodfall, Charles 93
Woodfall, Henry Snr 6, 10, 56, 86, 93, 97
Woodfall, Henry Jnr 93

Woodfall, Henry Samson 93
Woodfall, William 179-180
Worster, Benjamin 4, 10
Young, Edward 86